AN INTRODUCTION TO DIGITAL MEDIA

D0023680

An Introduction to Digital Media is a clear and comprehensive account of the development and future possibilities of digital media by one of their most authoritative analysts. Tony Feldman addresses fundamental questions about digital media and their potential use in our everyday lives. What are digital media? What is special about them? How do digital media systems work, technologically and commercially? And where is the digital media revolution taking us?

Tony Feldman considers the new digital media in two distinct but increasingly converging areas: the world of packaged 'offline' media such as CD-ROM and the world of transmitted media, including digital broadcasting and interactive online services. He begins with an overview of the digital media landscape, and goes on to describe the impact of CD-based media and the development of a consumer market for multimedia products. Feldman then traces the equally dramatic growth of online services and the Internet in particular, assessing myths and realities about the information superhighway and its commercial possibilities.

An Introduction to Digital Media concludes with an assessment of the strategic implications of going digital for media industries such as publishing, broadcasting, cinema and music, and considers the key role that individuals will play in determining the course of the digital revolution.

Tony Feldman, one of Europe's leading digital media consultants, is a founding director of the highly respected media and convergence analysts Informed Sources International. A prolific writer, his recent books include *Multimedia* (1994) and *Electronic Media Markets* (1992, with Julian Dickens). He also edits the authoritative European newsletter *Interactive Media International*.

AN INTRODUCTION TO DIGITAL MEDIA

TONY FELDMAN

A BLUEPRINT BOOK
PUBLISHED BY ROUTLEDGE
LONDON AND NEW YORK

First published 1997
by Routledge
11 New Fetter Lane, London EC4P 4EE

Simultaneously published in the USA and Canada
by Routledge
29 West 35th Street, New York, NY 10001

© 1997 Tony Feldman

Typeset in Garamond by Intype London Ltd
Printed and bound in Great Britain by TJ Press (Padstow) Ltd, Padstow,
Cornwall

British Library Cataloguing in Publication Data
A catalogue record for this book is available from the British Library

Library of Congress Cataloging in Publication Data
A catalogue record for this book has been requested

ISBN 0–415–15108–2
         0–415–15423–5 (pbk)

For Deb, Sam and Hannah

CONTENTS

FOREWORD

Writing about digital media is worse than painting the Forth Bridge. British readers will know the old story of the trials and tribulations of keeping the great bridge properly painted to protect it from the depredations of the Scottish weather. There is so much ironwork that no sooner has the paint dried on the last spar and buttress than the whole process has to begin again at the other end. Writing about the so-called digital revolution is like this but more so. No sooner has the ink dried than the words already written need revision. But not for the same reason that dooms those poor bridge painters to repeat the same exercise over and over again. Words lose their currency in this subject not because it takes so long to say them but because the technological and commercial landscape that they describe changes so swiftly.

This is probably a very bad way to start a book of any kind. It hardly instils confidence to say it is going to be out of date even before the printer has printed it. There is, however, a genuine way round the problem of delivering a static snapshot of a fast-changing subject. The current work, and earlier ones on which it is based, aim to deliver a foundation of material – ideas, insights and demystifications – which remain current far longer than the superstructure of detail which makes up the day-to-day helter-skelter of change. While sudden technological breakthroughs can, of course, upset the apple cart completely, it is broadly possible to sketch the logical geography of digital media so the result delivers (hopefully) some lasting value. Even *Multimedia*, the book published in 1994 which the current work effectively supplants, retains some of its original value because it presents underlying concepts which – while not quite eternal – are at least a fairly firm, long-term foundation for making sense of the bigger picture with all its plethora of fast-changing detail.

There is, however, a more subtle problem which is personal to any author writing in this field. Not only do the realities of technologies and their commercialisation change from day to day, but also our understandings of the implications of these processes change. Not only is the real world a moving target. So is our perception of it. The reason is simple.

No one has a monopoly on the understanding of what the headlong rush into digital media means. There are no real gurus, only a great many people grappling with what all the complex interplays of new technologies, new business models and new social responses to media and information add up to. The day of the expert is over. Everyone has a legitimate viewpoint and should feel confident enough to express it. What books like this one try to do, therefore, is not to dictate a point of view as if cast in stone but to think through what is happening and come up with some models for making sense of it. But a process of thinking it through – like keeping the Forth Bridge free of rust – is actually a task without end. In other words, if you do ever think you have reached a final conclusion, it is probably the wrong one! So a book like this one has to be the author's take on the world at a given moment in time. It is not only a snapshot of a real world of events and activity but also a snapshot of an internal world of mental models, ideas, perceptions and – it has to be admitted – doubts and uncertainties.

Few things spring new and fully formed into the world, least of all books like this. The immediate antecedents are obvious. In 1990, I was asked by the British Library to write a study in the British National Bibliography Research Fund series. The idea was to focus on a new word in the information and publishing industry and to examine what the term meant and what implications the technology embodying it contained for the publishing, bookselling and library community. The new word was 'multimedia' and the research study was eventually published in 1991 by the British Library under the title *Multimedia in the 1990s*.

The study began by reflecting that 'if the history of our technological age is just a flicker of time, then multimedia, amidst all the bustle of change is a word still forming on our lips. It is an embryonic concept in a fast-changing environment and we have to be realistic about the limits of our power to forecast or even speculate about its future'. Five years later, this book deliberately avoids using multimedia in its title because it has become both an over-used industry cliché and a false focus for our thinking. Yesterday it was a word still forming on our lips ready to take centre stage. Today it is just one word among the many we need to interpret the wide-ranging processes of change and development that are reshaping the media and information industries.

Within two years of its publication, I was asked by the British Library to revise the original study and the result was then published early in 1994 by the Blueprint division of Chapman and Hall as *Multimedia*. The new book – focused as it was upon offline, predominantly compact disc (CD) based multimedia – has rapidly grown into a mild anachronism. Not because it has entirely lost currency but because it treats CD multimedia as the important focus instead of placing it in its proper context as an important fragment of a much bigger picture. Consequently, even if this new work continues to owe some of its sections to earlier writings, it is essentially an attempt to sketch the bigger picture and to do so in simple, easily assimilable terms. It is a work of introduction rather than a definitive treatise. In presenting it, the aim is to shape a mental map of the digital media world which will be an aid to those embarking on all the varied journeys that people tend to take in their different sectors of interest and activity.

Because this book is motivated by a desire to demystify, to keep things simple, some compromises are made. First, the book does not pretend to be comprehensive. It sets out to provide the headlines and supporting explanation from many key sectors of the digital media world but it will not detail every avenue or look at the subject from every media orientation. Second, it may – from time to time – play fast and loose with technical rigour. The reason is that comprehension is higher on the agenda than the fine tuning of technological cause and effect. This is not a book about technology but about its implications and we need to understand technology only so far as that understanding accurately informs our insight into those implications.

Here is a thumbnail sketch of the book's structure. First, we consider what we mean by digital information in the first place and why it has the power to reshape our experience of media so profoundly. These are basic foundations on which all digital media activity stands. Next, we outline the digital media landscape by crudely dividing it into two broad sectors: offline, packaged media such as CD-ROM (compact disc read only memory), and transmitted media – both passive and interactive – delivered by a range of electromagnetic and physical pipes making up the different forms of digital networks. Then – just to confound this simplification – we show how offline and transmitted media do not exist in isolation from one another but are rapidly merging to create powerful, new hybrid channels of delivery. We look closely at the evolution of online electronic services and, in particular, study the rise of the Internet. A particular focus here is the commercialisation of the World Wide Web and which business models and technological infrastructures are emerging to make it possible. Finally, we end where perhaps we should always begin: with the customer, the only person who will ever pay the bill for all the human and technological resource deployed to make the digital revolution deliver the goods. The key question is what goods do such customers want to buy and how are they responding to the present outpourings of new media products and services? We look at today's realities and consider what may lie around the corner.

You will notice as – and if – you read on that there is a distinctly commercial emphasis throughout. The reason for this has nothing to do with value judgements about commercial motivations. It is merely a reflection of the fact that technology will do what it can ultimately do only if someone is prepared to pick up the bill. This is another way of saying that not everything that can be, will be. Although this is a simple and uncontentious proposition, much analysis of the digital future throws it to the winds in favour of a kind of intoxication, an undisciplined, unrealistic love affair with the potential of technological advance to deliver all sorts of wonders without considering whether those wonders carry with them any compelling commercial logic.

This is familiar territory because the idea that 'what can be, will be' is an established view of how the technological future will pan out. There is even a good pedigree for it. In the world of physics, for example, 'what can be, will be' is an established principle, understood as a fundamental characteristic of the natural world. Even if the event has only the tiniest probability of taking place – sometime, somewhere – it will take place. Things do not happen only if they are forbidden by a basic, underlying physical law. This has some disquieting but illuminating consequences. For example, the room you are sitting in is filled with molecules of air buzzing around at thousands of miles an hour, colliding with one another and bouncing about in a chaotic mêlée. There is – I fear to report – a tiny but finite probability that, as you read these words, all the molecules will suddenly rush into the far corner of the room, leaving you to die horribly of asphyxiation! The good news, however, is that the statistical probability of this happening, while not zero, is not much greater than zero. In other words, if you need cheering up, just consider that it is vastly more likely you will be run over by a bus than die through lack of oxygen through a statistically freak event. The point, however, is that the world of physics does not view such unlikely events as things that may happen but as events that will definitely take place at some time. Not only can the improbable happen, it will happen. If you wait long enough, the least likely things in the universe will happen. Those monkeys tapping away at the keyboards of their wordprocessors will eventually write the entire works of Shakespeare word for word. In other words: 'what can be, will be'.

This same principle, consciously or unconsciously, is often made a part of the logic of technology forecasting. We tend to believe that 3D television, virtual love making and matter transfer ('beam me up Scotty!') will arrive one day simply because we believe that the remorseless advance of technology will necessarily deliver it. In other words, if technology can do it, it will happen. This 'what can be, will be' principle works well in physics but is fatally flawed when we try to apply it to human beings and what they do with their society. For sure, technology must be capable of delivering 3D television and other wonders before we can have it. But it will emerge as a reality in our lives only if we are all prepared to pay for it. We will have it only if we want it enough to buy it.

In other words, the engine of change in digital media is not underlying technology in itself but clever technology married to customers prepared to pay money to enjoy the fruits of its cleverness. The key to creating the digital age, therefore, lies in the hands of those able to envisage ways of putting the technology to work to generate products and services that users will – whether they know it or not beforehand – want to buy. So commerce is good. Indeed, it is the only thing that drives the digital age forward.

The age itself is going to be one of radical change in our lives. After all, the way we experience information, entertainment and education shapes us as individuals and – on a grander scale – shapes the character of whole societies. There is justification, then, in talking about the move to digital media as a kind of revolution. However, one person's revolution is really another person's evolution. If events move quickly and carry dramatic change with them, they are likely to be called revolution. If the same events unfold more slowly and carry less obviously radical implications, they are likely to be called evolution. However, rapid or slow, the processes of change – all change – do not spring from sudden discontinuities of development, isolated breakthroughs with no link to anything that has gone before. Even if some events – a very, very few – which shape our technological world are stumbled upon seemingly by chance, the interpretation of that chance event and its eventual application is based on understandings that have been built up over decades, even centuries of previous technological development. So, however profound its long-term implications, the move towards digital media is far from being a revolution. It is happening quickly but is an organic process of development: a logical, step-by-step progress into an extraordinary new future. So extraordinary, perhaps, that we can talk about going digital as a process of evolution with revolutionary implications.

This is more than playing with words. Seeing digitisation as evolution encourages us to believe we can look ahead, even guide and influence the pace and direction of its impact on our lives. Evolution is predictable and is therefore something worth analysing. True revolution – if there is ever such a thing – is impossible to call. So, if we agree that we are presiding over digital evolution, we can at least take a stab at understanding where it is taking us and how it might get there. This book, after all, is worth attempting!

A fundamental belief in an evolutionary world returns us to the idea that books – like the digital age – are built on antecedents. Some of this book's past has already been outlined. But it is worth concluding with the antecedents that cannot be crystallised so easily. During the fifteen years I have been involved in digital media, I have learned an immense amount from industry colleagues. Many have been untiringly generous with their time, explaining aspects of digital media development that have been difficult for me to grasp. To all of those many people – past and present – all colleagues and friends in the same basic endeavour, I would like to express warm thanks and appreciation. I hasten to add that the good bits in this book are due to their aid and the errors and omissions are entirely my own responsibility!

I also acknowledge with thanks the kindness of my newsletter publishers. To Interactive Media Publications, thanks for allowing me to make some use of articles I have written for *Interactive Media International*, the monthly publication I have had the delight of editing with my valued colleague, David Powell, since 1990. To Pira International, similar thanks for permitting me to draw upon some of my regular contributions to their periodical, *Publishing Technology Review*.

Lastly, I must thank my children, Sam and Hannah, for reminding me daily that there is a sense in which the world is invented afresh every time the sun rises and that there is no end – nor should there be – to the pleasures of exploring and discovering that world.

Tony Feldman
London 1996

Abbreviations

ADPCM	adaptive differential pulse code modulation
ADSL	asymmetric digital subscriber loop
AOL	America Online
ARPA	(US Department of Defense) Advanced Research Projects Agency
BT	British Telecom
CCITT	(European Commission) Consultative Committee on International Telephony and Telegraphy
CD	compact disc
CD-I	compact disc interactive
CD-ROM	compact disc read only memory
DAT	digital audio tape
DCT	discrete cosine transform
DOS	disk operating system
DVD	digital video disc
ELDA	European Laser Disc Association
EPOD	European Platform for Optical Discs
FTP	file transfer protocol
GUI	graphical user interface
HARC	Houston Advanced Research Centre
HDTV	high-definition television
HTML	hypertext markup language
HTTP	hypertext transfer protocol
iKP	Internet keyed payments
IP	Internet protocol
ISDN	Integrated Services Digital Network
ISO	International Standards Organisation
ISP	Internet service provider
ITV	interactive television
JPEG	Joint Photographic Experts Group
MPC	multimedia personal computer
MPEG	Motion Picture Experts Group

MSN	Microsoft Network
NCSA	National Center for Supercomputing Applications
NTSC	National Television System Committee
NVOD	near-video-on-demand
OEM	original equipment manufacturer
PAL	phase alternation line
PC	personal computer
PCM	pulse code modulation
RTOS	real-time operating system
SSL	secure socket layer (protocol)
STT	secure transaction technology
TCI	Telecommunications Inc.
TCP	transmission control protocol
UKOL	UK Online
URL	universal resource locator
VGA	video graphics array
VOD	video-on-demand
VRML	Virtual Reality Modelling Language

CHAPTER 1

WHAT DIGITAL REVOLUTION?

We have already dispatched the idea of revolution and settled for seeing the move to digital media as a process of evolution with potentially revolutionary impact on our lives. But the word 'revolution' remains on all our lips. Leaving the semantics aside, what we are really expressing with the use of the word is not an analysis of whether digitisation is the result of a discontinuity in technological development but a less rigorous, general sense that something truly remarkable is taking place which is likely to transform all our lives and – perhaps, more profoundly – the lives of our children. The idea of digital revolution is implicitly an image of humankind stepping through a doorway into an unknown and fundamentally changed future. And it is a one-way journey, a doorway through which we can never step back to return to the comfortable media certainties of the past.

However, we need to begin any inquiry about the future impacts of digital media by understanding the starting point of the whole process. It can be summed up in a very few words. The digital revolution is being forged by an accelerating move from a world familiar with analogue media to a world that will be increasingly dominated by digital media. This, then, is the key – a shift from analogue to digital. To make sense of that simple statement, however, we need to know what analogue and digital mean and, most important, why they are different. After all, the revolution is in the difference.

ANALOGUE AND DIGITAL INFORMATION

A good way of getting a sense of what analogue information and digital information are is to imagine 'analogue' as an expression of our experience of the real world while 'digital' expresses a world belonging exclusively to computers.

Whether we know it or not, therefore, we are all familiar with analogue information. Typical examples of it are the continuously varying intensities of natural light, the meanders in an audio record's groove, the variations in an electrical current and the mechanical fluctuations in the air which we interpret as sound. The information embedded in an analogue signal therefore is always built into some continuously varying value which can be measured. By measuring it and responding to its continuous variation, we extract the information it contains. When we listen to music, for example, our eardrums vibrate with the rhythm of changing air pressure. This creates a signal in the auditory nerves which is interpreted by our brain as the pleasing notes of an orchestra. Vision is a response to changing values in the intensity and wavelengths of light on the retina of our eye and transmitted to our brain by our optic nerves for decoding and interpretation.

Another familiar example is an old-fashioned wristwatch. When we glance down at its face we see hands sweeping across the dial at various speeds. They move continuously, covering every part of the dial at some stage of their journey. We judge the time of day by the relative positions of the hands against the scale of hours, minutes and seconds printed on the watch face. This kind of information display is analogue. We read the message of our watch by looking at a constantly changing display. There are no gaps in the information. It is a continuous flow. This is the fundamental nature of the analogue world.

Digital information is different. Its character is essentially discontinuous. Far from reflecting continuously varying values, digital information is based on just two distinct states. In the digital world, things are there or not there, 'on' or 'off'. There are no in-betweens. Digital computers talk in a language called binary code. It consists of just two symbols, the digits 0 and 1. Everything a computer does, it does in this starkly simple language. Significance in the information is created by placing the symbols in different orders. In other words, the sequence 00011000 means something different from 00010100. A rich and powerful language is built up in this way. In computer jargon, each of these binary symbols, either 0 or 1, is known as a bit (a contraction of 'binary digit'). A character of computer information – the smallest information element carrying significance in itself – usually consists of eight bits arranged in a characteristic sequence. The overall sequence is called a byte.

To contrast analogue and digital information further, we can return to our wristwatch parallel. You can always tell when people are using a digital watch. Ask them the time and they will invariably say something like, 'It's 4.41'. How often do you really need to know the time to the exact minute? An analogue watch user will just glance at the timepiece and say, 'It's about a quarter to five'. In digital timekeeping it is always one time or another. It is never 'about' anything. However, there is an instant when a digital watch is speechless. When the display flashes from one second to the next there is a tiny gap in the information. So, although the watch seems to supply a constant and exact reading of time, it is in fact a discontinuous display sampling individual moments of time and displaying them.

It is worth noting that although today we take for granted that computers are entirely digital, it was not always so. The earliest electronic computers were actually based on the measurement of analogue quantities. For example, an analogue computer would do its sums by passing an electrical current of a known value across a wire which would put up a known amount of resistance to the passage of the current. Because a basic law of physics tells us that voltage is always the result of multiplying the size of a current by the resistance of its carrier, we can effectively perform a simple multiplication just measuring the voltage across the wire in the computer. This simple idea of measuring related analogue quantities was the basis of analogue computing and it worked. But it worked slowly and laboriously. Digital computers are vastly more efficient. They work by just measuring whether electronic switches or 'gates' inside them are either open or closed. The condition of either being 'open' or 'closed' creates the two distinct states needed for binary code language. Adding up numbers in this way – which is all computers really do – is dramatically faster than stitching together calculations by trying to measure currents, resistances and voltages thousands of times every second. Indeed, today's most powerful machines can process millions of instructions every second to carry out the behest of their programmers. In other words, digital computers are not merely fast. They are faster than we can possibly imagine.

So – although it was not always true – today when we go digital, we are speaking the exclusive language of computers.

SPEAKING THE LANGUAGE OF COMPUTERS

Why is the distinction between analogue and digital information so important in digital media technology? The answer lies in what you can do easily with digital information that you cannot readily do with its analogue counterpart. In other words, the digital revolution is founded on the distinctive characteristics of digital information that set it apart from the real world of analogue experience. The unique features of digital information are the key to its commercialisation and, ultimately, to its potential impact on our lives. What, then, is uniquely special about digital information? There are five key factors.

- Digital information is manipulable
- Digital information is networkable
- Digital information is dense
- Digital information is compressible
- Digital information is impartial

DIGITAL INFORMATION IS MANIPULABLE

By taking information out of the analogue world – the 'real' world, comprehensible and palpable to human beings – and translating it into the digital world, we make it infinitely changeable. In the analogue world, the reshaping of a page of information or a physical object requires some exercise of brute force. Usually, however careful we are, the change inflicted causes damage. The process is difficult, slow and untidy. More important, if we take something apart in the real world it is often difficult, if not impossible, to put it back together again.

If we translate analogue information into a digital form, however, we translate it into a medium which is infinitely and easily manipulable. We are able at a stroke to reshape the information freely – whatever it represents in the real world – in almost any way we wish and we can do it quickly, simply and perfectly. Then, when we are ready, we can reconstitute and display it as new information which human beings can once again perceive and comprehend.

An important point here is not merely the inherent manipulability of digital information in itself but the fact that digital information has this manipulability at all stages: from the moment it is created or captured in digital form to the moment it is delivered to its user and beyond. In particular, consider the significance of media being manipulable at the point of delivery because it suggests nothing less than an unprecedented new paradigm for publishing and media distribution.

The fact that media are manipulable at their point of delivery means something quite extraordinary: users of the media can shape their own experience of it. This means that manipulable information can be interactive information. We will examine the notion of interactivity in more detail later (pp. 13–17) but for now it is enough to understand it as a means of providing a dynamic experience, one which is controllable and influenced by its user's own preferences. Potentially, for example, a new generation of interactive products will offer users a way of finding their own path through material or of tackling it at a pace that suits them or of retrieving what they want quickly by making cross-referenced searches or important correlations. This is a dramatic contrast to the traditional passive, linear experience of media that characterises the analogue world. And it suggests a powerful new model for publishing and media distribution. To understand why, consider our past experience of media products.

Until the arrival of digital media, publishers and distributors of information, education and entertainment have enjoyed a single great privilege. They have been able to dictate what customers will view or read with only a modicum of selectivity left to the customer's discretion. Television scheduling has created the notion of 'channels' and ensured (give or take the intervention of video recorders) that certain programmes will be viewed and at certain preordained times. The same is true of radio. More fundamentally, both the television and film industry are founded – very successfully – on linear storytelling models. In other words, their products are created to be viewed in a particular sequence, usually embodying a beginning, middle and an end. Whether or not it would make sense to do so, viewers have had no way to re-order the sequence of programming – rather like mixing up the chapters of a book – or to select prime bits from it.

In the world of book and periodical publishing, customers buy the whole product even if all they want – and actually use – is one small part of it. In the old analogue world, customers had no freedom to say: 'We like your book but we really only want chapters 3, 8, and 10. May we have – and pay – for just those please?' The publishing model has always been one of benign tyranny. Publishers tell their customers not only that they must buy the entire contents of a printed work but also that they must have it paginated, designed, illustrated and bound exactly in the manner the publisher decides.

This dictatorial model is so firmly established in our experience of media products, it is unquestioningly and uncomplainingly accepted. In the digital age, while old models are unlikely to be swept away totally, new models will emerge which will alter our expectations for ever. Increasingly, users of media will find the power to control media experiences shifting in their direction. While, of course, originators and publishers will continue to determine the constraints within which this new found freedom is experienced, there is no doubt that the old model will ultimately come under pressure from the new.

A good example of how this process is already happening is the creation by McGraw-Hill in the United States of a customised, on-demand publishing service called Primis. Essentially it allows teachers to select in 'mix and match' style material from a wide range of existing McGraw-Hill publications plus other third-party materials and order a bespoke textbook made up of parts of those materials. Chapters from one book can be mingled with chapters from another and additional commentary and analysis can be supplied through articles extracted from journals or other publications. Teachers can even inject some of their own original work to be combined with the already published material. The result is a highly customised new text suited to an individual teacher's needs. This remarkable new approach to educational publishing was not the result of a radical vision on the part of McGraw-Hill. It was an approach effectively forced upon them by an establishment of educators which was taking increasing exception to the high price of educational textbooks. This culminated in the emergence of a fast-copying business in New York which began to supply photocopied, bespoke collections of proprietary published texts to teachers tired of paying heavily for material only partially relevant to their needs.

McGraw-Hill took the photocopiers to court for breach of copyright. The result was a technical victory for McGraw-Hill but a storm of bad publicity. In response to establishment pressure, McGraw-Hill determined to build a legitimate publishing operation – using digital technologies – that attempted to meet the expressed needs of its customers. In doing this, it demonstrated its understanding that in the changing world, media companies – whether they like it or not – must listen and be responsive to the wants of their customers.

Whatever the future prospects of Primis or its immediate derivatives, the new model of customer primacy is established and – as interactive technology makes it an increasingly practical proposition – responsiveness to individual customer requirements will become a vital issue for media companies of all kinds to grasp.

Digital information is networkable

This means that information in digital form can be shared and exchanged by large numbers of users simultaneously. And because networks can be global in scope, the individuals doing the sharing and exchanging can be geographically dispersed. We will look at network developments in more detail in chapter 5 but it is worth noting some important, immediate implications.

Simultaneous access to networked information means distributing the same underlying content product many times over without the difficulties and costs implied by shifting physical products through a supply chain. In other works, networks transform the economics of media distribution. Networks can also offer the capacity for users not only to communicate simultaneously with a body of information but also to communicate among themselves. This means that networks are good distribution conduits but are also a means of creating a new form of electronic community, a grouping of people whose geographic location is irrelevant and who are instead drawn together by the common thread of the network they all use.

Digital information is dense

We can squeeze a lot of information in digital form into a small physical space. Much depends, of course, on the particular storage technology used – some offer greater storage density and capacity than others – but there is little doubt that immense practical convenience can be gained from the compactness of the digital format. The most obvious example is the portability of a compact disc – a technology we will examine in detail in chapter 3. If we use a print-on-paper analogy, we can encode the contents of a small library on a compact disc and mail it around the world for the cost of a postage stamp. More specifically, not only text but also digital images and video can be squeezed on the disc. Until networks emerge routinely able to handle such big files quickly, the discs will be the easiest way of transporting multimedia from one physical location to another.

DIGITAL INFORMATION IS COMPRESSIBLE

If digital information – dense as it is – is not dense enough, it can be compressed to get even more into the same physical space. As we will see when we examine digital video technology in more detail, the single most important ingredient in making it possible to handle video in digital environments is our ability to compress the digital files involved and then decompress them when needed.

The technology of digital compression is a complex, technically challenging field but it is one of the single most crucial technologies driving the transition from analogue to digital media. What it does is to effectively make narrow information pipes fat. We are not talking here about physical pipes necessarily but any kind of conduit for carrying information from one place to another. The electromagnetic spectrum, for example, is a pipe that has long been used by radio and television broadcasters to deliver their content to customers. Although the spectrum is not a physical channel of distribution it has one of the general characteristics of a pipe: it has a limited capacity for allowing information to flow through it. This analogy with pipes and their physical capacity is merely a means of making concrete a key notion in digital media. The fatness or thinness of our pipes for carrying information define a quantity called bandwidth and bandwidth itself is the real determinant of how much information we can convey to people and how fast we can send it. In other words, if our pipe is narrow it has limited bandwidth – we would call it a narrowband transmission or distribution channel – and we would struggle to send large quantities of information through it at any kind of pace that makes sense to its users at the other end. If our pipe is fat, it has much greater bandwidth – a broadband channel – and we would be able to transmit a great deal of information very quickly.

Before the digital age and the emergence of digital compression technologies, we were largely stuck with the various pipes we had, whether those pipes were wires or cables in the ground – or in electrical equipment – or vibrations of electric and magnetic fields shimmering across a spectrum of wavelengths. All had different bandwidths but were what they were – narrow or broad. Digital compression changes all that. Instead of fiddling with the pipes to find more capacity, we can for more or less the first time fiddle instead with the information we propose to send through the pipes. So, by compressing digital information, we can effectively render thin pipes fat and fat pipes fatter. That is the miracle of compression and it has transformed our ability to handle large bodies of digital information over transmission systems such as broadcast and one-to-one networks and around the insides of computers. In particular, it has single-handedly made it possible to include video information – a medium which requires the processing and transfer of huge files of data – within complex digital environments. This single fact has transformed our experience of computing, reshaped the capabilities of computer networks and is soon going to rewrite the future of the entertainment industries.

DIGITAL INFORMATION IS IMPARTIAL

Computer systems do not care very much about what bits and bytes – the building blocks of digital information – actually represent. They care even less who they belong to. As far as a computer system is concerned, a bit is a bit and a byte is a byte and so long as the zeros and ones which underpin binary code add up to something comprehensible to the computer, it will do what it is told with them. While this is a deliberate simplification of the complex rules which actually govern the workings of computers it serves to make a crucial point about digital information. If the great flux of zeros and ones does not care what individual bits and bytes actually represent in the real world so long as they are properly constituted for the digital one, digital data can represent any form of underlying information. This means that digital information can be multimedia information.

This single idea has driven a revolution in thought about the uses of computing of all kinds. While in the early 1980s, most people's link with the computer was a blinking cursor and a capital C on a blank screen, prompting them to key in some arcane coded messages to get the computer to do something useful, today's personal computer (PC) users take for granted graphical interfaces such as the Macintosh system or Microsoft's Windows to help them run programs and get value from their systems. But the possibilities of multimedia have gone a major step further than this. Beyond the interface is the real substance of computing and multimedia has injected into this the possibility of enriching programs and digital content with sound and images of all kinds – including video. And, of course, the enrichment of human experience that this implies does not have to be delivered by computers that look like computers. It can also be offered by 'plug and play' devices for the home with an output often suitable for playing back through the television. In other words, a range of black boxes aimed at a mass market with computers tucked away inside them can offer the same powerful deployment of multimedia – perhaps for entertainment and education in the living room – as desktop computing can in a different, rather less friendly and less accessible context.

COMMERCIALISING ELECTRONIC MEDIA

If these are the unique qualities of digital information – or at least, the most important ones from a media viewpoint – then the commercialisation of digital information, entertainment and education services and products is based on finding a successful interplay of these features that delivers a package of benefits that customers will want to buy. There would plainly be no point in television going digital, for example, if all customers received as a result was the same programming, the same visual quality, delivered in the same fashion and at the same price. Better to stay in the analogue business and not bother. But if going digital can offer benefits that users will pay more to receive – greater choice of programming, more freedom to choose what they want to watch when they want to watch it, higher quality reception – then digital television offers a commercialisable opportunity for television companies. There is similarly little value in turning perfectly good words on a printed page into electronic images, sounds and words on a computer screen unless the process adds discernible value to the experience of using the underlying content. Electronic books, magazines or newspapers cannot just be books, magazines and newspapers in electronic form. The process of going digital must mean that their print-on-paper counterparts are transformed into a new medium with substantial unique, added values.

And this is the key to all electronic publishing endeavour, whether it is the delivery of traditional television programming or the development of a new generation of digital books, magazines and newspapers. The unique characteristics of digital information have to be put to work to deliver new benefits to customers – benefits they will recognise as benefits and be prepared to pay for. Whether enough of them can be encouraged to pay a high enough price, determines whether or not the digital media publisher has a profitable business.

We can easily illustrate the idea by looking in more detail first at the industry we still call television and then, by contrast, at the world of book publishing. In both cases, we will see how different features of digital information are deployed to create commercialisable benefits for customers.

The television industry is on the brink of being transformed in a very specific way by the shift to digital transmission. While in the long term, going digital will pave the way for the first high-definition television (HDTV) standards, in the immediate future digitisation will allow television broadcasters to compress their signals and – as we saw above – effectively increase the fatness of the transmission pipes they own or to which they have secure access. For example, let us concentrate for a moment on the direct-to-home satellite television industry where the impact of digital compression is already being felt. A satellite broadcaster probably spends currently £4 million to £5 million a year to lease time on an analogue transponder of a satellite. Transponders are the devices which effectively accept an incoming signal from an Earth station and retransmit it (usually at a changed frequency) to dishes positioned on the roofs of viewers' homes, schools and offices. A typical satellite has traditionally carried about 18, each capable of handling a single analogue television channel. So 18 transponders mean – in most cases – 18 channels of television programming per satellite. A restricted amount of bandwidth by anyone's standards and a capacity that certainly does not meet current demands of hopeful channel broadcasters who want to put more viewer choice into the skies. Heavy demand and low capacity, of course, add up to high leasing costs.

The shift to digital transmission dramatically changes the picture. Going digital for the satellite television industry means an opportunity to commercialise the compressibility of digital data. In other words, out of the menu of five unique features of digital information, satellite television is so far selecting one and putting it to work. By compressing the signals, the narrow pipe arbitrated by satellite transponders can be substantially expanded. Instead of each transponder handling a single analogue television channel, they will soon be routinely capable of handling up to about 30. In practice, the increased bandwidth created by compression can be utilised in different ways. You can, for example, squeeze either 30 channels of poor visual quality television through a transponder or a single channel of ultra high quality. The practical reality will probably be that most transponders will handle about 18 channels. But this is a spectacular enough piece of broadcasting arithmetic because it means that a satellite that could once offer 18 channels via 18 transponders can now offer 324. Given the schedule of new satellite launches over the next few years, digital compression could be offering European viewers literally thousands of individual channels by the turn of the century.

Seen on a channel by channel basis, this is almost overwhelming capacity and suggests a substantial lowering of leasing prices, offering a changed economic model for satellite broadcasting which could open the industry to many non-traditional broadcasters. Satellite transmission could soon become an increasingly effective way of delivering a whole new range of core content ranging from in-store information systems for retailers to data feeds for corporate networks – both applications which are already emerging, even in the present analogue age. The commercial reality for consumer applications, however, is that much of this available bandwidth may be taken up with broadcasting that has little to do with individual channels – the old model for the television industry. Massive slices of capacity instead will be utilised to create satellite television's answer to interactive services.

Satellite television is fundamentally different from television delivered by cables in the ground. While there is considerable tension between these two industry sectors in Europe over which of them will dominate the digital future, it is clear that cable television, based as it is on a physical link with its customers, is better positioned to create a return path for its customers to use than satellite. A return path is the fundamental requirement for interactivity and has never formerly been an issue in television. The reason is simple: television and television technology have always been based on a broadcasting model. In other words, television has always worked by sending everything to everyone. Viewers could select what they watched at any given time by tuning their receivers appropriately but that did not alter the fact that all viewers were sent the same signal containing the entire television offering. In this model, a return path is neither present nor required. However, if you want to turn broadcasting – a point-to-multipoint communication – into the one-to-one communication needed for interactive services you must have a good return path for one party to tell the other what it is they want. Such one-to-oneness offers the prospects of services – in this case, television-related services – on demand. In other words, individual viewers can ask for any service out of a choice of offerings at the moment they wish to have it. And they uniquely will receive it.

The massive expansion of satellite bandwidth offers the satellite television industry a means of creating a simulacrum of this on-demand opportunity using as a return path nothing more elaborate than a telephone line. The new model remains a broadcasting application but instead of broadcasting a single channel once it is broadcast many times over, gobbling up the available bandwidth with the repeated transmission. In practice, the approach can consume anywhere between 75 and 150 channels' worth of capacity. The most obvious use is in creating the semblance of a video-on-demand service. In this case, this is the same selection of video titles broadcast over multiple channels but not identically. Each channel's transmission is staggered slightly so that a certain video starts slightly later on one channel than on the next and so on across the range of channels utilised. What this means is that subscribers to the service can indicate via a telephone line – a transparent process managed by a special kind of set-top box – that they want to buy a viewing of a particular programme and then switch to the channel on which it is next starting. By using a large number of channels, maximum wait times can be reduced to as little as a few minutes. So, while not a true on-demand application requiring full, one-to-one interactivity, a service utilising bandwidth this way provides a potentially 'good enough' near on-demand experience. Not surprisingly, the application has come to be known as near-video-on-demand (NVOD).

We have laboured these processes of change in the television industry because they perfectly illustrate how a single unique capability of digital information – its compressibility – can be turned into a powerful new commercial opportunity. It is, of course, more than merely a commercial opportunity for television companies. It holds within it the seeds of pro-found change. It is the launching pad for a multichannel future for all kinds of television broadcasting with immense implications for companies trying to preserve competitive advantage, channel identities and hard-won brandings. For the television industry, therefore, digital compression alone – quite apart from the other characteristics of digital information – is a real touchstone for revolution.

If we now look at the turmoil facing the print-on-paper publishing industry, we see a more complex picture emerging. Publishing is an indus-try on the brink of change and development based on every one of the key characteristics of digital information we listed earlier. First, the manipulability of the information is being utilised to create a new gener-ation of interactive, highly searchable education, reference and entertain-ment products. Second, underlying information is being increasingly delivered by publishers over public computer networks. This network-ability is itself being used in two broad ways. It is allowing publishers – including some who have never previously been considered publishers – to create new forms of distributed publications – such as electronic journals – that exist only on the networks. And it is also being put to work to create a new distributed model of traditional publishing by getting the networks to deliver information to remote printers where it is converted into analogue print-on-paper products. This process often goes beyond merely changing the point at which printing gets done by also allowing the products to be customised and delivered on-demand so customers get exactly the book, magazine or journal they each individually want, when they want it. Third, compact discs are being used to carry interactive products with the density of digital information ensuring that huge bodies of information are – where appropriate – embodied on a single disc. Fourth, compression is being used to add digital video to such products. Fifth, the multimedia capabilities of digital information are being put to work to enrich underlying 'book-like' information with a synthesis of sound and images. In other words, every one of the unique attributes is being utilised in different, sometimes closely related, ways to generate both threats and opportunities for the traditional publishing industry.

In reality, of course, to examine the impacts in two media industries in this way is a gross simplification. While it is true, say, that the television industry is going to be radically changed by the commercial implications of digital compression, those television companies with content assets – like publishers – are faced with the prospect of new ways of exploiting that content across networks, on compact disc media and by whatever other means digital technology offers. And not only raw content but also brandings can be consolidated and extended by deploying them in new media sectors where television has never formerly trod. This is really saying something very simple about the future of all forms of media exploitation in the future.

Consider the traditional sectors and how they have always referred to themselves. Organisations call themselves – and understand themselves to be – *television* companies, *record* companies, *book*, *magazine* or *newspaper* publishers. In every case, they identify themselves explicitly by the physical form in which they have always delivered their products. If there is only one thing going digital means, it is an end to such limited self-definitions. To survive and flourish in the new age, media organisations will have to understand their businesses in a broader context, defining themselves not in terms of any single means of delivery but as exploiters of content wherever content can viably be exploited. And that will mean across many different platforms and channels of delivery.

WHAT IS INTERACTIVITY?

It is clear from our analysis so far that digital media do not have to be interactive in order to revolutionise an industry sector. Leaving aside new generations of hitherto unprecedented products and services, digitisation also offers important opportunities to deliver traditional, linear information and media experiences in new ways. The added value lies not in the inherent character of the product so much as the manner in which it reaches its customer. However, interactive media – while only part of the bigger picture – are grabbing the headlines and capturing the imagination of media publishers and originators – if not yet entirely of users. Interactivity, the argument goes, offers the potential to create a new era in information, entertainment and education. Through interactivity, once dull, passive experiences will be transformed into something infinitely richer and more compelling. Interactivity, it is said, opens a new door in human experience, one that may even eventually supplant traditional linear media offerings.

Interactivity is so much woven into the fabric of much digital media development that we will not focus on interactivity in itself very much in the pages that follow. Instead it will feature implicitly throughout our assessment of various forms of digital media design, development and application. It is important, however, given the claims made for it, to outline what interactivity is and why it can be such an important building block in some – if not all – successful digital products.

Interactivity in an information system gives the user some influence over access to the information and a degree of control over the outcomes of using the system. In practice, this usually means that, in one form or another, the system presents the user with choices. The decisions taken influence the path the user follows through the information. Each decision point is rather like a crossroads. After reading the signpost, users move off in the direction of their choice until they arrive at the next crossroads. In a digital information system, multimedia or otherwise, the 'crossroads' and the resulting network of possible pathways are created by a computer program designed to control and moderate the user's access to the information.

Although interactivity of this kind places some control over access and outcome in the hands of the user, the degree of control is strictly limited by the computer software providing the interactivity. The software determines how many crossroads there are, where they are located and how many options are offered by each of them. All possible pathways are therefore defined by the design of the software. The user simply selects available options based on what the user wants to get out of the system and communicates them over some form of return path. For example, choices may be driven by a search strategy with the user seeking a particular item of information. Or instead it may be an unstructured, browsing investigation, as much a reflection of the user's curiosity as a desire to locate anything particular. In an educational application, the user may be firmly channelled by the controlling software into pathways that suit the particular didactic purpose of the application.

There is little really new in the notion of interactivity in electronic media. From the earliest moments of the electronic publishing industry, electronic databases have been accessed by means of search and retrieval software. The design of the software, coupled with the internal structuring of the database, define the interactions that users can have with the database. In other words, interactivity is really just another word for the ways in which a user can search and browse through an electronic database, the process being more or less constrained by the control software. The same, of course, is true whether the database is made up of text or of text combined with images and sound.

The real difference in designing interactivity for multimedia lies in multimedia's added richness and complexity. To design a means of navigating effectively amongst thousands of images, video sequences, sound, text and numerics, all seamlessly combined as a single information resource, is a challenging problem and one that lies at the heart of successful multimedia applications. Indeed, interactivity largely defines the user's experience of a multimedia product. After all, the content and potential benefits of such a product will be irrelevant if its users do not find the means of accessing it easy-to-use, powerful and compelling. In other words, interactivity brings a vital element of added value to all electronic information, whether multimedia or not. The degree of added value is determined by two main features: the design of the interactivity and its implementation.

DESIGNING AND IMPLEMENTING INTERACTIVITY

Designing the interactivity means programming the number and location of the 'crossroads' in the database, establishing the decisions that a user can take at each of them and determining the consequences of those decisions. A form of interactive access to databases which is having a major impact in digital media design more generally is know as hypertext. Strictly, the term applies to textual databases. When used with multimedia it is often adapted to 'hypermedia'. It is also becoming an important aspect of network development, being a fundamental underpinning of the protocol defining a subset of the Internet known as the World Wide Web. We will look at these concepts in more detail when we examine the technology of multimedia and examine the rise of the Internet in chapter 5. But whatever exact name we use for it, the basic approach of the original hypertext model applies. Users of information and media can follow trails that interest them by activating pre-embedded software links in the material they are using to take them from one idea or item of information to another associated one.

The implementation of interactivity involves two key issues. First, the information system must work. This means putting the software, hardware and data in a practical and reliable configuration. For example, consider an application involving an interactive video system. There would be no point in designing software to control access to a video disc, unless suitable interfaces are also available to make it possible for the computer in the system to communicate with the video disc player and control its operation. At this level, therefore, implementation is an issue of system integration, making sure all the elements, software and hardware, communicate and function in an appropriate and concerted way.

The second issue focuses on how the user interacts with the information system. In other words, what kind of interface exists between the user and the database? At a mechanical level, the interface may be a keyboard and a screen. At a design level, the interface determines the screen design and its functionality. When using a computer, the most important kind of interface is the one that sits between the computer user and the computer's operating system. The operating system is the fundamental software brain of the machine which allows it do things like process, transfer and store information. So the way we get at the operating system effectively defines our experience of using the computer. It gives us power over the machine. If it is easy to use and powerful in the degree of control it gives us, it is a good interface. If it relies on knowing complex and unnatural command languages which have to be laboriously typed into the machine, it may well be powerful but will also be forbidding and difficult to use, a real barrier to ordinary human beings getting the best out of computing. The most successful type of interface today is known generically as the graphical user interface (GUI) and is so widely established today that it is easy to forget that as recently as the late 1980s, many people's experience of an interface between themselves and an operating system was merely a flashing cursor and a 'C' prompt on an otherwise blank screen.

The first widely used, commercial GUI was the one designed by Apple in the early 1980s for their Macintosh range of computers. The Macintosh user interface has been called the first 'intuitive' interface, suggesting that a user can learn how to use it by instinct alone without the need for instruction manuals or training. The design of the interface is based on its use of what have become known as 'real-world metaphors'. For example, the underlying metaphor for the working space on the screen is a desk top. Data files are visually represented by on-screen icons, designed to look like tiny office files. Unwanted files are removed by being deposited in a dustbin icon which even bulges to show that something has just been put in it. The full power of the Macintosh interface and, indeed, all GUIs, however, runs much more deeply than the clever choice of icons. It is the overall functional design which creates the attractive combination of power, convenience and ease of use. For example, the icons are usually addressed by inputs from a mouse rather than a keyboard and many of their operational facilities are controlled by pull-down menus. More recently, GUIs also incorporate a windowing facility enabling users to create a window within one application through which they can simultaneously run another. The most overwhelmingly successful example of this form of interface, of course, is Microsoft's Windows, now used by nearly 100 million PC users worldwide. In its Windows 95 version – launched in summer 1995 – the software for the first time went beyond being a mainstream interface alone riding – as it did in the past – on the old DOS (disk operating system). Now Windows is an interface and operating system seamlessly combined. The processes of computing and interacting with the real world have at last combined and – with huge benefits in speed, usability and basic functionality – the interface has been drawn into the heart of the computer itself.

The future of interface design, however, may well hold radically different approaches to solving the problem of getting human beings and computers in touch with each other. So far, all interfaces have been based on a single very silly notion. They have been created to allow clever people to communicate with dumb machines. The new paradigm for the twenty-first century must surely be to turn this on its head. In other words, the future lies with interfaces that allow dumb people to communicate with clever machines. While what we have today suffices – so long as people are prepared to work hard to learn how to work the modern generation of intefaces – what we really need to turn computing into mainstream appliance technology, as familiar and usable to a 7-year-old child as to a 37-year-old computer enthusiast, is intense development work not on interface design but on computer intelligence. Once we can build computers that really understand who we are and what we want and can respond to our spoken requests and physical gestures, we will truly have created the ultimate interface: the same one we have as a species used for centuries to communicate amongst ourselves. Within the next 50 years this kind of computing will arrive and those of us who are alive to see it will look back in astonishment at the age of Windows and other graphical interfaces and marvel that we spent so much time and trouble in the early years of computing, trying to solve the wrong problem.

Whatever revolution in human computer interaction the future holds, we must deal with what we have in the present. This brief discussion of interfaces only touches on their significance. The important point to emphasise, however, is that the design of interactivity in digital media systems, including the choice of user interface, fundamentally affects the experience of using them. This means that the effective design and implementation of all aspects of the interactivity is crucial to the success of interactive media.

CAPTURING HEARTS AND MINDS

Interactivity has become a largely unquestioned gospel in many sectors of the digital media industry. The reason is simple. Interactivity is one of the most spectacular, unique features which digital media offers. Because the potential 'non-linearity' of digital media is one of its most powerful advantages over traditional, linear media such as film or video, it is hardly surprising that its proponents promote interactivity as a vital ingredient. But an advantage has significance only when it is used to advantage.

In *The Challenge of Multimedia* (1992), an Infonortics research study written a few years ago, British multimedia expert Patrick Gibbins echoes a common line in the multimedia industry claiming 'the more interactive an application is, the more it will engage the user's interest and attention'. While few would question that to capture interest and attention is crucial to the long-term success of any form of media, experience so far suggests that interactivity often has exactly the opposite effect. Instead of capturing interest and attention, interactivity becomes too much like hard work and makes users switch off, mentally and physically.

This is, of course, a generalisation. In practice, there is much that is effective and attention-grabbing in current interactive media design. However, the successes are most often scored in applications which have a high procedural element and with users who are strongly motivated to put effort into their experience of using the new media. The best interactive training applications, for example, are instances of this.

Elsewhere, there are signs that interactivity can be too demanding for some people's taste. While interaction allows a remarkable degree of user control and independence, it also demands thought. The problem facing multimedia designers is to create underlying designs which make the inter-activity so painless and transparent that the user is aware only of its benefits.

In the field of consumer multimedia, in particular, designers need to find some compelling way of engaging the imagination of their customers. Examine the current range of multimedia offerings and you will find little that touches your feelings and nothing that really moves you. The sad fact is that we have not yet learned how to make interactive media work upon our emotions. Why is this such a *sad* fact? Because the key to the great popular success of traditional media has lain in their capacity to engage in a cohesive, spellbinding process of storytelling. By contrast, the interactiv-ity in interactive media so far has tended to fracture and fragment the stories the media have tried to tell. Imagine Steven Spielberg making an interactive disc with hundreds of pathways through thousands of images. What chance would any one person have of stumbling upon the exact sequence that produced the movie *ET*? In other words, interactivity eman-cipates its users but runs the risk of giving them so much power in determining their own experiences of content that the only message con-veyed is the one the user chooses to create. The freedom to chart your own course, therefore, can emasculate as readily as it can liberate.

Of course, we may not always want to make the users of interactive media laugh or cry. But if we believe that one of the keys to popular success across a range of sectors is winning customers in their homes, then we need to entertain them as convincingly as television, video and the movies. This means capturing their imaginations by touching their feelings as much as their minds. We must be able to create the equivalent in interactive media terms of the book you cannot put down. We need to create experiences that grip and linger.

We should not underestimate the problems of meeting this great chal-lenge. After all, the conventions and internal structures of traditional media which today we take for granted, have taken decades or even centuries to evolve. Perhaps the full impact of interactive media in our lives, therefore, must await the evolution of a new creative language, one we are at present only just beginning to glimpse.

DO WE NEED INTERACTIVITY?

For many, the shift to digital means a move from passive to interactive media. But it is already clear from what we have said about how digital media are being commercialised that interactivity is only a single thread in the fabric of change and development. It is obvious by simply reviewing the kinds of digital media activities already underway worldwide that the 1990s and beyond are years in which traditional media industries will be trans-formed as much by new ways of delivering their old forms of products as by the rise of radically new paradigms. And interactivity is assuredly radical – both in what it demands of media originators and publishers and in the kinds of impacts that it has on customers reared on an unvarying diet of passive, linear information and entertainment.

So what role does interactivity have in the new, digital world? It depends, of course, what we mean by interactivity. Clearly, the degree of choice available to customers in the multiplatform, multichannel future will demand a degree of interactivity just at the level of navigating the data flow. If all the information and entertainment in the world are somehow easily available to us whenever we want them, the prospect adds up to something worthwhile only if we can find what it is we value and shut out the rest. And – while it may be some time before everything becomes available – the huge amount of media content soon to be piped into our homes, offices and schools by a variety of technologies will add up to a daunting and potentially overwhelming tidal wave. The only way to search the digital flux quickly, and return with what we really want, is to use computer software that can conduct the search and retrieval operation on our behalf. Such 'electronic pairs of hands' can sift the untold mountains of digital media to select exactly what we want, when we want it, only if they are told in the first place what to look for. So, not only will we need to manipulate the electronic search process, but also we will need to know what we want before we set it in motion.

If this sounds familiar, it is because it is exactly the same process that underpins the sale of data via online databases, an electronic publishing sector that is already over 30 years old. We will look at the online industry in more detail in chapter 5 but for now it is worth noting that in that industry the search and retrieval process was a major stumbling block to development and growth. And it was a problem because search and retrieval was a difficult process to control. You needed to be an expert to handle the software effectively. There was a good reason why the software was difficult to use. The online databases were big and complex. To run powerful searches you needed powerful search software. And powerful systems inevitably tend to be complex and difficult to control. The flight deck of Concorde, while actually a masterpiece of ergonomic design, is overwhelmingly complex to the untrained eye. But it is not complexity for complexity's sake. Concorde is a complex piece of engineering. It does a lot of clever things and to fly it safely needs every bit of complexity on that flight deck. Einstein once said that 'things should be as simple as possible, but no simpler'. In other words, control has to be related accurately to purpose and experience teaches us that in the design of any kind of control system, ease of use is usually inversely proportional to the power of the system being used. As what we try to do gets more ambitious, so the tools for doing it get more difficult to use. One of the greatest design and development battles facing the digital media industry, therefore, is to make the complex, powerful computer systems on which the industry relies, not just simple to operate, but trivially so. We need to find a means of making the technology transparent so that all the user sees is its application.

What does this mean in terms of our immediate digital future? One thing it suggests is that even in cases when the digital products delivered are no more than the same old analogue ones but with added value in the way they are distributed, there will be serious interactive design issues to be addressed just to ensure users can find what they want. Otherwise, increased customer choice rapidly becomes a bane, not a boon. Navigation software must give customers an easy-to-read, easy-to-use road map of everything they can have, so they can get what they want with no fuss and definitely no prior training. If it is only a partial map, if it is inaccurate, if it is hard to read – the new world of abundant media choice will fall flat on its face. So interactivity and interactive design counts in a big way even when it is only a pathway to linear experiences.

More generally, of course, interactivity is generating new forms of media products which rely fundamentally on interactivity as the basis of their appeal. The 'need' for interactivity in these cases is self-evident. But the degree of interactivity, and how it should be blended with other ingredients of design and which will engage and satisfy users, is a complex subject intimately dependent on assessing the individual objective of different interactive applications. We can attempt here only a few general comments to indicate some important themes.

In applications such as education, training and corporate information products, it is relatively easy to specify what is required by users. A set of requirements can literally be written down on a piece of paper. With that kind of blueprint, it is a straightforward matter to design a product to match the needs of its market. The level and nature of interactivity, therefore, fall quite naturally out of an analysis of market requirements. This makes the process sound more simple than it is and the capacity to get things wrong remains. However, publishers who do get this kind of product development wrong do so for culpable reasons: they have not bothered to understand their market well enough, they have decided they know what is best for the market rather than the other way round, they have specified the requirements badly and created the wrong product, they have specified the requirements perfectly but made a 'pig's ear' of the design, or they have allowed technical errors in the underlying program so the product is unreliable or – it has been known! – simply does not work.

In the entertainment sector, life is very much harder. Specifying mass market games or so-called infotainment and edutainment products – which are meant to combine pure fun with something more cerebral – is a hard and unrewarding task. One of the problems is that no one quite knows what sells in this market and people are reduced to talking in meaningless phrases, a kind of new age marketing babble. New products are said to be 'rich, compelling learning experiences', 'multilayered information systems, alive with sound and images' or 'virtual worlds where you live or die by the quickness of your wits'. To be fair to publishers and originators in these fields, they are faced with an impossible task. All that the glib phrases really reveal is a huge uncertainty about what makes these kinds of products sell. Unlike a business product where a quantifiable, readily articulated need is being addressed, in the entertainment sector publishers work largely on a wing and a prayer. Sometimes it is a very heartfelt prayer because the upfront investments in leading edge products can run into seven figures. Of course, it is possible to introduce a little science into the process by examining the track record of other products, running focus sessions with consumers and buying tie-ins with big name media brands or other bankable associations such as blockbuster movies to boost a new product's prospects. But the underlying reality is stark. Consumer market products remain a major gamble and blending appropriate levels of interactivity with the other ingredients is more a task for instinct, flair and good luck than it is for measured, scientific judgement. The business model that flows from this is simple. You produce ten titles and hope the two that succeed compensate for the eight that fail. You try to learn from the mistakes but can never hope to realise every consumer publisher's dream: the ability to publish just the two successes. Perhaps one day we will understand how interactivity fits into the picture more clearly than we do today. But for now and for a long time, the use of interactivity is just another element of what remains, at best, an expensive gamble.

CHAPTER 2

MULTIMEDIA

This chapter is not going to attempt an overview of multimedia as if it was a distinct sector of digital media. Instead, it will offer a working definition of the term and then focus on a crucial area of media technology development: the techniques of digital compression and how – in very simple terms – they work.

WHAT IS MULTIMEDIA?

It may seem odd to bother with a specific definition when we have already implied one in chapter 1. But multimedia is an ever present word in the language of digital media and it is worth – even briefly – making sure that when we use it we all mean the same thing.

The history of definitions of multimedia is an interesting story in itself and while we will not spend much time on it, it is worth looking back at some very early efforts just to illustrate how tough a task it once seemed. In 1990, for example, when the word was only just becoming common-place, the Information Workstation Group's study, *Micro Multimedia*, suggested:

> Micro multimedia is multimedia supported by a microprocessor(s). It uses multiple media data types. The Information Workstation Group definition requires the presence of graphics or natural images unless Micro Cinema is present. The use of audio or numerics with text does not qualify as multimedia. The presence of text or numerics is optional. Motion is not required. Interactivity is not required ... Programmed passive experiences can be multimedia ... Materials excluded from micro multimedia include: television receivers where the end user can not effect [*sic*] the onboard computer programming, CD-V (linear play), programmable digital watches with graphic displays and audio alarms.

There is more, but just this sample suggests the deep and unintelligible waters it is easy to fall into when trying to be explicit about multimedia. The British magazine, *Multimedia: computing with sound and motion*, published in the same year by EMAP, apart from attempting a definition in its own title, also took a much more robust approach to defining multimedia in its first editorial:

> Multimedia is all things to all people. The name can convey a highly specific meaning or less than nothing, depending on your audience. In fact, multimedia is a singular mix of disparate technologies with overlapping applications in pursuit of a market and an identity.

This may have been true at the time but if multimedia was really in search of an identity, it is a curious irony because at the time and for some years afterwards, multimedia suffered from having rather too many of them. In their excellent evergreen *CD-I Designers' Guide* (McGraw-Hill 1992), Signe Hoffos together with Dr Graham Sharpless, Phillip Smith and Nick Lewis make this point in the course of their own struggle with definitions:

> The word multimedia has already acquired diverse meanings in various technical fields. Some computer buffs use multimedia to describe the hardware which allows computer data to be sent from one machine to another. Many audio visual specialists remember when multimedia meant presentations which combine still images from slide projectors with a soundtrack. Some software producers use the term to describe packages which combine computer-generated text and graphics on the same screen, especially if the graphics move or there are sound effects.

Hoffos and her team eventually find at least part of the solution to defining multimedia by describing it in terms of the technology that delivers it.

> Ideally, multimedia systems provide in a single box, all the hardware and software necessary to combine still and moving pictures – including video, photographic images, computer graphics and animation – with sound, text, computer-generated data and computer programs. Equally, all the information in a multimedia programme – sound, pictures, text and data – can be recorded on a single object (typically, an optical disc).

There is, of course, a final option in the definition game. Avoid tackling the issue directly and offer context instead. In his study, *The Challenge of Multimedia* (Infonortics 1992), Patrick Gibbins tries this tactic with some success, refusing to be drawn into explicit definitions and arguing that the meaning of multimedia will become clear in the context of the study. But, however tempting it is to take this easier route, and true though it is that context does indeed support understanding, we obviously need to do our best to pin the term down more firmly. If we allow multimedia as a term to remain shapeless and subjective, how can we ever hope to have a common basis for understanding its implications for the information industry and the generations of information users who may (or may not) benefit from it?

A useful starting point is to go back to the 1970s to a time when computers were still huge, unfriendly devices demanding air-conditioned environments and costing millions. Even if desktop computing had not yet been invented, the term 'multimedia' was already in use. In the world of educational publishing, in particular, multimedia meant kits, typically a combination of pupils' booklets, teachers' guides, film strips, audio tapes, and photographic slides. Such products, attractively boxed and delivered to the classrooms of the early 1970s, certainly offered multiple media – text, images and sound – but each was delivered as an independent element in the package. The different media were fragmented, difficult to integrate. Welding them into a single resource for classroom teaching was a difficult task for the teachers and a confusing, unsatisfactory experience for pupils. Despite a strong commitment to resource-based teaching at the time, most schools found multimedia kits more trouble than they were worth. Most were commercial failures and publishers quietly dropped them and returned to textbooks, the monomedia which had always been the core of their business.

We could spend much time analysing the possible reasons for the failure of classroom multimedia in the 1970s. One clear reason, directly relevant to our pursuit of an identity for multimedia, concerns the way in which the different media were being presented. Although excellent in themselves, each of the elements of the multimedia kit was delivered independently. This fragmentation was, of course, unavoidable. In the mid-1970s, the technology needed to bind the individual media together simply did not exist. There was no way of combining the information in the workbooks, the sounds of the audio tape or the images of the slides and film strips. In the mid-1990s, however, the multimedia environment is dramatically different. Electronic technology provides a single medium with the power to integrate diverse types of information. So the first stage of identifying modern multimedia is to focus on its power to draw together different forms of communication, smoothly integrating them within a digital environment, and providing access to the stored information using computer systems which are fast, friendly and, above all, interactive.

We now have an identity for multimedia, a working definition against which we can measure developments and potential impacts. We can describe multimedia as follows:

'Multimedia' is the seamless integration of data, text, sound and images of all kinds within a single, digital information environment.

By 'seamless' integration we mean so close an interweaving that the discrete character of the different types of individual media is submerged in the experience of the multimedia application. The idea of the integration taking place within a digital environment is crucial but does not of course imply that non-digital information cannot play an important role in multimedia, only that such information needs to be digitised and brought into the common environment. Hybrid systems using part-analogue, part-digital information will not survive in the long term. Pure analogue systems – such as traditional video discs, for example – are a technological dead end.

Why such uncompromising emphasis on the common environment being a digital one? We have already offered an answer in chapter 1. Only if multimedia is digital can it be enriched by the unique features of digital information which are themselves what are driving the profound and comprehensive changes in the media industries which we have touched on earlier. Being able to apply these unique features to multimedia, of course, serves to define multimedia's ultimate power, impact and scope of application. Quite simply, multimedia, lying at the heart of electronic media development, can have no serious future unless it is also digital.

DIGITAL VIDEO

The defining technology of multimedia is digital video. Or, more precisely, our ability to handle full motion video information within a digital environment. This ability is based entirely upon one technique – the technology of digital compression. But before considering briefly how the processes of compression work, it is worth framing the reason why video itself presents such a technological challenge to digital media systems.

The simple reason is that once video goes digital it takes a huge amount of digital information to describe it. The problem is related not only to the complexity of rendering a high quality colour image but also to the demanding task of keeping up with the continuing rapid changes of image that characterise the way video delivers its impression of on-screen motion.

The exact amount of digital information needed to represent video depends largely on the quality of resolution with which the images are rendered. In a computer environment, screen displays are made of thousands of illuminated pixels, points on the screen which can be individually illuminated to form a viewable image. By refreshing the pixels with new instructions, images can be made to change and if they do so sufficiently quickly, one result can be animation, computer-generated motion.

There is a straightforward relationship between the resolution of a particular type of screen and the amount of data needed to support that resolution. For example, one of the standard monitor resolutions now widely used in computing is called VGA (video graphics array). A typical VGA screen consists of 640 pixels across and 480 pixels down. This means that a screenful of information is provided by 307,200 illuminated dots. The quality of resolution depends not only on this absolute number of pixels but also on the number of colours and intensities which can be utilised at each pixel. The data needed to provide this colour/intensity control are provided in the form of a bit code. Codes based on a higher number of bits can deliver more colours and intensities than those using very few bits. In the case of VGA, the size of the code is typically four bits for each pixel. In other words, every two pixels accounts for one byte of information. At VGA resolution, therefore, a static screenful of information needs 153,600 bytes (153.6 kilobytes).

Now let us look at television information and gain some sense of the amount of data needed to represent motion video. In the United States and Japan the system of encoding analogue television signals is called NTSC (National Television System Committee). It defines a television image in 520 horizontal lines of information, updated 60 times each second. In the UK and most of Europe, the PAL (phase alternation line) standard is used. Although similar in concept to NTSC, PAL uses 625 lines updated 50 times each second. Each update in fact provides half a frame of information. Since television pictures are built up by interlacing two half-frames, the factor of 50 updates per second means that the picture is updated at 25 complete frames each second. The horizontal resolution along one of the PAL lines is equivalent to about 700 dots, each a separately luminescing spot on the cathode ray screen. This means that a screenful of PAL television is represented by roughly half a million dots. Translating the colour quality required into digital terms means that each of these dots has to be addressed by the equivalent of 16 bits of information. Therefore 25 frames per second equates to around 20 megabytes of data every second. This is the rate of data transfer needed to produce television quality video in full motion on a full screen. Even a single, still image at this quality requires about 800 kilobytes of data.

It is worth noting – because it is a widely exploited feature of PC-based multimedia – that it does not have to be like this. We can drastically reduce the amounts of data involved by simply cutting the size of the video image. If full screen video needs around 20 megabytes a second, quarter screen video needs only 5. Reduce the image further and you similarly cut the data load. You can go further. We saw in the arithmetic above that a major ingredient in fuelling the data load is the fact that video data are refreshed at 25 frames per second (in Europe). If we sacrifice both frame rate and picture size, we can cut the data load still further. Indeed, the degree of sacrifice may not be great. After all, if 25 frames per second represents what is technically described as full motion, would the eye of the consumer really notice a drop to 20? In practice – depending on the video footage involved – digital producers can go as low as 15 frames per second and still retain much of the quality of full motion, even if the video gets a little jerky when the action hots up. If you want to take risks, you can also cut the data still further by reducing the amount of colour data in the images and making do with a grainy greyness instead of sharp, contrasty video quality. A trade off among frame rate, picture size and (possibly) colour resolution, therefore, can substantially reduce the technical demands of digital video. But the Holy Grail remains the effort to deliver full screen, full motion at good quality resolution.

Compromises aside, the huge amounts of information needed to convey images such as full screen colour stills or full screen, full motion video represent one of the greatest challenges for multimedia technology. The problem is both one of storage and processing power. It may be more of one than the other, depending on the approach of the multimedia system. For example, in the sector of the multimedia industry focusing on compact disc media, even the huge capacity of the disc looks modest compared to the demands of video. A compact disc – for all its hundreds of megabytes of storage space – could hold only about 30 seconds of uncompressed 'television quality' full screen video. And even if we wanted to store such a short segment, we could never get it off the disc fast enough to replicate full motion. The rate of data transfer needed would be well beyond the maximum capabilities of most compact disc systems. This is a problem of storage and transfer. As far as delivering the end product is concerned, somewhere in the chain a powerful computer is needed. In the 1980s, multimedia could never have been a viable industry simply because most of the computers of the day were not powerful enough for the job. And those that had the power were far too expensive to be used except in specialist, high value applications. But today multimedia can address a big audience because its principal delivery technology is widely and cheaply available. In simple terms, desktop computers of the late 1990s – and appliances based on the same underlying technology – are now powerful and cheap enough to deliver multimedia quite routinely to millions of people all over the world.

While multimedia in general needed to await the arrival of affordable computing power to deliver its fruits, digital video within multimedia relies foremost on techniques of compression which squeeze huge digital video files down to more manageable size and then allow the same files to be decompressed at the point of delivery.

COMPRESSING DIGITAL INFORMATION

Data compression techniques are not special to multimedia. They are simply a much more urgent requirement than in most other areas of application. The benefits of data compression have always been obvious. If a message can be compressed one hundred times, it can be transmitted in one-hundredth of the time, or transmitted at the same speed through a channel with one-hundredth of the bandwidth, and it can be stored in one-hundredth of the volume of the original. Of course, the message will make sense only if it can be successfully decompressed when it reaches the user. Although this analysis is not strictly accurate – there is always a compression/decompression overhead of about 5 per cent – the benefits and potential cost savings are substantial and compression techniques have been a major field of development from the time of the very earliest digital databases.

Although a full analysis of compression techniques is beyond the scope of this book, it is important to emphasise that a large number of proprietary compression schemes are now available, most conforming to underlying world standards established and internationally agreed in the early 1990s. While we will not dwell on the technicality of such schemes, compression is of such great significance in the development of digital media, it is important to touch on some key ideas.

COMPRESSION BY REDUNDANCY

One of the most important approaches to compression is to exploit the inherent redundancies in information. The simplest example of redundancy is to imagine a personnel record held in a computer system. If you use 'M' and 'F' to denote male or female in the gender field of the record, you require eight bits of data to represent either character. If you decide to replace the characters with an agreed, fixed-length one-bit code, you immediately achieve an eight to one compression of the gender field. This kind of simple redundancy occurs widely in databases and a significant level of compression can thereby be achieved through little more than an exercise of common sense and ingenuity.

In the case of images, considerable redundancy can be found simply by locating parts of the image that are the same. The basic technique is called run length coding and works by replacing a long run of unchanging data by the shortest possible code. For example, imagine a television picture, one-third of which is showing a uniformly blue sky. In digital terms, the sky would normally require about 0.4 megabytes of data. However, a massive compression can be achieved by creating a relatively short code of just a few bytes which effectively tells the computer that 'the next 400,000 bytes will be blue'. The short code would then be acted on just before display to produce the appropriate number of blue pixels to represent the sky.

This concept underlies a technique for compressing video which has become vitally important in multimedia. The basic idea is extended, however, to keep track of a constantly changing picture and to detect only those elements in it which change. Typically, for example, a modern compression scheme will work from a sequence of 'reference frames' throughout the video sequence. These reference frames are encoded in their entirety. The only additional information stored is the video information that changes between each of the consecutive frames. The rest is thrown away. The most widely used compression schemes based on this process discard well over 90 per cent of the original video information and still manage to reconstruct good quality footage. In cases where there is plenty of fast action such as sports coverage, however, such compression schemes are placed under real pressure simply because they cannot keep up with the levels of change taking place between reference frames. Although they are constantly being refined, the basic approach of compression through throwing information away – known picturesquely as 'lossy' compression – is obviously fundamentally limited. You can never throw away more than everything and once you are discarding over 95 per cent of the original video information, you are touching the limits of what can be regenerated – at acceptable quality – from so little underlying data.

For all its obvious limitations, however, lossy compression now dominates media development in all sectors where compression is important and is commonly applied in a format called MPEG (after a team called the Motion Picture Experts Group) which has effectively become the world standard for video compression schemes.

Audio compression can also be achieved by identifying acceptable levels of redundancy and stripping them out. For example, digitising an analogue sound signal requires the repeated sampling of the analogue waveform. The value of the different levels arising from each of the samplings are turned into a bit code. Reproducing a smooth waveform in digital code requires a very high rate of sampling every second, particularly if the wave is complex with many different component frequencies. However, because the wave is being represented by discrete sampling operations, the digital representation will be a 'stepped' shape rather than a continuous smooth curve. The more samples taken, the smoother and less stepped the representation will be and the better quality of the sound. One way, therefore, of reducing the digital data is simply to reduce the number of samples taken. This works but quickly leads to reduced quality. Practical compression techniques try to cut the data with the minimum effect on quality. Most serious work has focused on improving pulse code modulation (PCM) – the basic method of breaking a waveform into discrete elements for digitisation – and on the transmission of the bit codes that measure the value of the waveform. An important variation known as adaptive differential pulse code modulation (ADPCM) is today widely used as the basic compression standard for much CD media development.

Data compression is so vital to the future of information media that considerable international efforts have been made to create global standards governing the way in which compression is handled. The standards administered by the International Standards Organisation (ISO) will eventually form the basis of all multimedia video communications services and publishing covering Integrated Services Digital Network (ISDN), satellite and terrestrial broadcast systems, local area networks and storage media such as magnetic hard disc, optical disc and digital audio tape (DAT). Each of the standards initiatives seek a common method of compression based on the discrete cosine transform (DCT) process which will ultimately assist the process of authoring multimedia for a range of different platforms and help to building underlying inter-platform compatibilities.

Although we will not examine the technical aspects of these standards, it is important to identify briefly the most important initiatives. There are three. First, there is a standard that applies specifically to videoconferencing. It is called H.261 (or, sometimes, px64) and has been formulated by the European Commission's Consultative Committee on International Telephony and Telegraphy (CCITT). It came into force as an international standard during 1991. Second is the Joint Photographic Experts Group (JPEG) which has now created a standard for compressing still images (although it can also be used for video). The third is called the Motion Picture Experts Group (MPEG). As its name suggests, MPEG defines a standard for coding moving images and associated audio.

COMPRESSION IN HARDWARE AND SOFTWARE

Although MPEG is now a widely accepted standard and, in its original and evolved forms, is likely to shape the future of all kinds of multimedia delivery, it is only one basis for compression and remains a very demanding one, particularly at the level of playback. In other words, while it is relatively easy and cheap to create MPEG files from analogue video masters, it is still hard to find the computing power in personal computers to decompress them for end users to enjoy. What is needed in most computers is a special set of chips designed to do the grunt work on behalf of the host computer. Currently such cards cost a few hundred dollars to buy and are far from easy to install and use. In other words, they remain gadgets for enthusiasts rather than the mainstream of media and information users.

None of this matters if you are selling multimedia via a proprietary set-top box or stand-alone multimedia player. While these are computers of a kind, they are not general purpose devices. They are specifically created to decode and deliver digital satellite broadcasts, for example, or to play videos or video-rich interactive games from a compact disc. In other words, these devices are proprietary systems customised to a particular commercial purpose. The creators of these systems can ensure that they handle MPEG decompression by simply supplying them with the appropriate chips built into them. In the case of general purpose computers, by contrast, specialised chips sets add cost to the product to deliver a facility only a few at present may wish to use. In other words, a computer manufacturer is likely to include MPEG decompression as a routine feature of its products only when full screen digital video is a routine prerequisite of the desktop computing market.

From a multimedia publisher's point of view, MPEG can be utilised in products only if the means to decompress the MPEG files is readily and widely available. In the world of digital television, the commercial battleground is initially focused on the struggle to get appropriate MPEG-based set-top boxes into enough living rooms to create a market for digitally compressed television. In compact disc multimedia, proprietary systems such as CD-I (compact disc interactive) offer on-board MPEG decoding but need to establish a large enough installed base of users to make the video software market viable. Multimedia aimed at personal computers – usually delivered by another form of compact disc usually called PC CD-ROM (compact disc read only memory) – can address a very large potential audience but with very few machines equipped with the special chips needed to make sense of MPEG.

But MPEG is really important only where full screen, full motion performance is crucial. In applications where something less is tolerable, MPEG and its problems can be laid aside in favour of less demanding solutions. For partial screen, reduced frame rate video specialised software engines are now widely available which allow most PC users to decompress video files without having to modify their hardware in any way. The best known of these programs are Microsoft's Video for Windows, Apple's QuickTime and Intel's Indeo. They all offer the same prospect for a multimedia publisher – the opportunity to sell the razor with the razor blade. In other words, a publisher can include video files in its product compressed by one or other of the proprietary software schemes. To make the video accessible to customers, the publisher adds the decompression software to the multimedia product. When the customer installs the product for the first time, the decompression software automatically transfers itself to the host machine's hard disk and waits, ready to go to work as soon as any video files are accessed. From a commercial publishing point of view, the advantages of this kind of software-based scheme are obvious. You do not have to rely on users to have special chips inside their computers. You do not even require them to acquire the particular decompression software needed for your offerings because you give it to them as a part of your publication. And the whole process is transparent to your customers and therefore is friendly as well as efficient. But the disadvantages are obvious as soon as the video files are retrieved. While software schemes can sometimes deliver excellent results, to do so they must rely on a very powerful PC. These are, of course, increasingly becoming the norm, but publishers still have to direct their publishing towards some kind of common denominator and right now that usually means configuring the playback software to run on fairly modest machines. This in turn means that the resulting video tends to be of relatively poor quality, covering only a small window on the screen. Good enough – if the video is chosen carefully – to enrich a consumer title but far from adequate if video is to be the centrepiece of the product.

It is interesting to speculate on how this situation might change. Mainstream computers are getting increasingly powerful. Even home users are buying top end machines. In 1994, for example, in the United States more Pentium-based machines were sold for use in homes than in the large corporations for which they were originally expected to be destined. As this trend gathers pace, the common denominator of software-based video performance will be capable of working the software systems very hard indeed. Video windows will get larger, frame rates will rise to full motion and colour resolution will improve dramatically. At the level of PC multimedia, there is now a contest growing between hardware-based solutions to MPEG and the ability to decompress good quality video in software. Indeed, it seems likely that by 1988 or 1999, mainstream host machines – those PCs in widespread and common use – will be powerful enough to decompress MPEG in software alone without any special chip set to support them. At the same time, MPEG will anyway become cheap and compact enough to include routinely on the motherboards of PCs or within the silicon of their central processors whether purchasers particularly want it or not. One way or another, therefore, MPEG is well on its way to becoming a widely used standard for handling digital video within PCs.

This means that whatever may happen in detail at a technical level, the direction is clear. We are moving towards a widely available facility to include full screen video on computer screens as naturally as we have come to expect it from television screens. Perhaps even more pressing a question now is how well such compression schemes will allow the easy transfer of video over computer networks relying on ubiquitous but inherently narrowband links such as telephone lines.

MAVERICK COMPRESSION SCHEMES

Despite improvements in the software-based schemes, they are principally a pragmatic solution to a commercial publishing problem rather than a realistic way of handling extreme video compression. However, there are some mavericks seemingly challenging the power and influence of MPEG. In the early 1990s, for example, the most important of these was a system called fractal compression, based on the then highly fashionable new mathematical development known as chaos theory. Fractals are fundamental redundancies in the natural world – the detailed layers of repetition in the structure of physical objects, for example – which enable quite complex formations to be described very simply. This same principle was applied by a US company called Iterated Systems to produce a software-based compression based on fractal mathematics. Although an immensely powerful means of compressing image data – used, for example, to good effect in the early editions of Microsoft's Encarta CD-ROM encyclopedia – its competitive advantage has declined in the face of other software schemes. The great weakness of the fractal scheme was not in the principle on which it was founded or on its ultimate performance. It was the fact that while it was easy to decompress fractal data it remained difficult, time consuming and expensive to compress the data in the first place.

This relationship between the ease of compressibility and decompressibility is crucial to determining the commercial viability of compression schemes. MPEG, for example can now be compressed in real-time with fairly modest computers. This means that one hour of linear video will take an hour to compress. This makes MPEG nowadays a 'symmetrical' compression scheme. Asymmetric schemes like fractal compression are always less attractive because of the commercial need to get compression done quickly and cheaply.

But other new compression developments are emerging which could yet turn the world of data compression on its head. For example, in 1995, the Houston Advanced Research Centre (HARC) in the United States announced that it was on the point of commercialising a new form of compression based on a mathematical technique called wavelet analysis. The scheme – known by its originators as HARC-C – essentially reduces descriptions of image data to terse mathematical formulations. These alone are then transferred to the delivery device either via a network or CD-ROM system and the original image information is reconstructed at the users' end by their computer. The key to HARC's promise lies not in the fact that it uses wavelet analysis – many research teams had been working on this for some years – but in the apparent ability of the new scheme to work with computers of modest performance. It therefore looks like a scheme that could be commercially exploitable. If it lives up to the promises of its inventors – and, at the time of writing, HARC-C still has to demonstrate its claimed potential in commercial applications – it could soon be challenging MPEG as the dominant form of video compression. It offers some startling prospects. For example, it is claimed that it can deliver MPEG quality video over ordinary telephone lines with the software decompression algorithm included in the signal. This means that anyone receiving it could decompress the video because the can opener would be sent with the can. Ultimately, of course, MPEG is probably secure in the medium term because of its established position in the orthodoxy of world standards but – whatever happens to HARC-C in the bright light of the market-place – unexpected developments like it always need to be factored into any assessment of future compression developments and what they will be able to deliver in media terms. In other words, in this abstruse and highly mathematical sector of the digital media industry, it is as well to expect the unexpected.

One thing is clear. Comfortable assumptions of the recent past about MPEG's universal dominance, and the fact that it would necessarily be hardware-based, are now being fiercely challenged. The medium-term reality looks more like a world in which no single scheme dominates but a rich variety have influence in different sectors of application. MPEG, for example, is likely to be the de facto standard in the field of digital broadcasting while proprietary software-based schemes such as advanced variants of QuickTime, HARC-C, Duck Technology's Truemotion and software implementations of MPEG hold sway in CD-ROM publishing and online multimedia.

CHAPTER 3

THE COMPACT DISC ARRIVES

This chapter sets in motion a massive but useful simplification which we will use to structure the rest of this book. We are going to pretend that the digital world is a simple place where there are essentially two forms of media. One kind is more familiar than the other. This is 'offline' media, packaged in a stand-alone physical form, palpable to the real world and dominated by developments in optical disc technology in general and compact disc technology in particular. The other realm is transmitted media – abstract and invisible, where information is delivered via different forms of networks ranging from largely non-interactive broadcasting systems – radiating the same information from point to multipoint – to heavily switched systems which provide the uniquely one-to-one routeing of information which characterises interactive networks.

In practice, you cannot separate offline and transmitted media so easily. It is a convenient division but increasingly the realities of the market-place are creating a marriage of the two, combining their strengths in a powerful merger of technologies and publishing models which we will touch on at the close of this chapter.

Sometimes, however, it is helpful to pretend the world is simpler than it is – so long as you never forget that it isn't!

THE BEGINNINGS OF OPTICAL MEDIA

Before we examine the rise of the compact disc, we should spend a moment to reflect on its immediate antecedent, the video disc. Although it has much apparently in common with compact disc media, the original form of optical disc differed in one fundamental way. It was an analogue medium while compact disc took the same underlying technology into the digital age.

In the early 1980s, at the same time that the first home computer boom was at its height, the LaserVision video disc was exciting considerable interest as a publishing medium. It is not hard to see why. LaserVision (originally a proprietary name coined by Philips and, today, known generically as 'laser disc') emerged from the laboratories of Philips in the late 1970s. It is based on encoding multimedia information on the reflective surface of a silvered 12-inch disc. The encoding is done by a fine laser beam burning a series of microscopic pits into the disc surface. During playback, another laser beam passes over the surface of the spinning disc, acting as a stylus made of light. The way the light beam is reflected from the surface of the disc is affected by the presence of the pits, areas where the reflective surface has been burned away during the original encoding process. This modulation in the laser beam caused by the varying reflectivity is itself detected, decoded and reconstituted as the original multimedia information. Using this process, full motion, full frame video can be delivered together with the full range of other media types – still images, high quality sound and animations.

There are none of the problems of digital image data we have discussed in chapter 2 because the video disc is not digital. The laser beam, reading the pit code on the disc, is affected by the varying length of the pits. This creates a continuously changing value, characteristic of analogue information.

Although not a digital medium, the video disc is nonetheless the starting point for modern interactive multimedia development. There are two main reasons. First, a standard disc offers up to 55,000 frames of information, each with its own unique electronic address or frame number. This makes it possible to access any individual frame by calling up that address and displaying its contents. Second, because the disc offers radial access to its contents, an individual frame or sequence of frames can be located and retrieved very quickly. The combination of these two factors means that by placing access to the disc under computer control, it is possible to create an interactive multimedia experience. Contrast this with efforts to use a linear medium such as videotape interactively – the only other interactive alternative in the late 1970s and early 1980s. Even with careful design, the time taken to wind a tape back and forth to locate required information makes it laborious and frustrating, even in the simplest applications.

The computing muscle used for rapidly locating and retrieving required information from the disc is supplied either by a separate microcomputer linked to a laser disc player or a microprocessor built into the player itself. Software suitably designed for the particular application is employed to control the user's interaction with the multimedia data on the disc. This means that the choices a user makes determine the particular pathway that the user takes through the multimedia information, with the computer drawing as required on the text, sound, still images and moving video stored on the disc. Used this way, the video disc is no more than a peripheral to the computer, much as any external disk drive might be. It is simply a physical source of stored, displayable information, accessed by a computer as a part of an interactive product designed for a given purpose.

The manufacturers of video disc players in the late 1970s and early 1980s had high hopes for commercial success across consumer, professional and business markets. The reality has fallen far short of these early expectations. Although we cannot properly analyse the fortunes of the interactive video industry here, we can at least summarise. The only substantial markets for interactive products have proved to be in dedicated applications. In these, video discs have been commissioned to address a single, bespoke purpose rather than to provide a product speculatively for a wide range of possible customers. Generally, these bespoke applications have been in the fields of industrial and professional training and in experimental retail promotion such as point-of-sale and point-of-information systems which – on the whole – have gone nowhere.

It is too soon to say, however, that the video disc should be consigned to the scrap heap of technological history, particularly since the above comments relate only to applications offering significant degree of interactivity. In 1992, the European Laser Disc Association (ELDA) published sales statistics showing a remarkable resurgence in Europe of consumer market interest in largely linear playback of feature films and music videos.

This came as no surprise to Japanese and US video disc companies. Figures for their markets show substantial growth in consumer sales during the early 1990s. In Japan, for example, manufacturing figures for players rose from 500,000 in 1987 to nearly 1.3 million in 1991. Of the 1991 figure, about 550,000 were exported, mainly to the United States. The Japanese consumer market in 1992 had the choice of about 10,000 generic titles, most published by leading hardware manufacturer Pioneer. In the United States, the installed base of players has grown from 120,000 in 1988 to just under 300,000 in 1992. More recent statistics show a continuing substantial use of video discs in the US and Japanese markets. By the end of 1994, the total US consumer market stood at 1.5 million players with annual hardware sales holding steady at around 280,000. There were over 8,500 titles available. In Japan, the installed base of players had reached 4.7 million by the end of 1994 with annual sales running at over 400,000. The total number of consumer titles stood at nearly 18,500, mainly feature films, popular music and karaoke.

In Europe – in a move that speaks volumes – ELDA recently transformed itself into the European Platform for Optical Discs (EPOD) and now acts as a trade clearing house on marketing-related matters relating not only to video disc markets but the full range of CD media. Despite its change of name and orientation, the organisation continues to report surprisingly strong installed base figures for linear playback hardware. The figures for 1993–4 look like this (all figures are thousands):

	Benelux	France	Germany	Spain	UK	Italy	Rest of Europe	Total
End 1993	16	200	42	72	16	28	23	381
End 1994	18.5	230	48	126	22.5	29	29	484.5

These are not huge figures for a long-established technology, however, especially when compared, say, to Inteco Corporation's estimate for PC CD-ROM drives in European homes. At the end of 1994, Inteco reckoned that 2.7 million European homes had such drives, up from 360,000 the year before. But while video disc hardware markets are not growing fast, they are still growing. As the hardware base edges upward, sales of software are also rising. EPOD reports the following releases of new titles in Europe in 1994:

	Film	Classical music	Pop/jazz	Total
France	629	563	221	1,443
Germany	396	568	221	1,205
UK	204	548	191	963
Spain	169	568	196	948

Sales overall were up over 12 per cent in unit terms over 1993 with 2.3 million discs selling in 1994 compared to just over 2.0 million the previous year. However, these healthy-seeming numbers are heavily skewed by the efforts of a single Spanish publisher called Planeta Spain which has had an extremely successful time selling a package of hardware and software door-to-door. On its own, Planeta Spain contributed about half the total of European unit sales of discs during 1993 and 1994.

Currently, in Europe as in Japan and the United States, title catalogues are dominated by linear entertainment product. In other words, the video disc's survival seems to be based on its qualities as a high performance playback medium offering the best in sound and video combined. The competitive issue in the consumer market for digital media such as the new interactive CD multimedia platforms – and in particular, the forthcoming high density CD formats – is therefore not content and functionality but the fact that another demand is potentially being made on the all-too-limited consumer purse.

Old and non-digital as it is, video disc technology is – at the time of writing – still the only widely available platform available that can deliver high quality, full motion, full frame video complete with a range of trick frame features such as forward and backward variable speed motion and perfect freeze frames. As well as offering excellent interactive video potential in itself, it continues to provide a useful stored source of video imagery for use in real-time digital video systems using digitising interface adapters. While the future may well belong to thoroughbred digital systems, right now it is a question of satisfying today's needs with today's technology. Superior as the unified digital environments for multimedia may be, right now they simply cannot deliver high quality video in a form you can easily buy. New high density formats will be arriving in the market during 1997 but will initially be expensive. In addition, a potential format war is likely to confuse consumers until – like VHS video and Betamax – the market-place works out what it wants. The promise of high quality, feature length video in digital form is certainly there but, for the moment, if we want such video to use today in linear and interactive applications, we still have to compromise on the digital ideal. Of course, you will have to want interactive video quite badly because interactive video discs and their players are costly. So, as far as interactive applications are concerned, video disc still looks like an answer in search of a question that can afford it.

It is of course only a question of time. Video discs have a brief window of opportunity remaining before the digital video discs and interactive high density compact disc media cut the ground from beneath them. The analogue video disc is not yet quite dead but it is certainly dying. The future, therefore, is digital and that means the dominance – in various flavours – of compact disc technology.

HOW DOES A COMPACT DISC WORK?

While we do not want to delve deeply into underlying technology, it is worth giving at least a brief account of how a compact disc works. We have already touched on the basic principles when we examined the rise of the video disc and we cover similar ground again here but with the profound distinction that while video disc technology is an analogue media system, the compact disc is digital.

The old fashioned gramophone is a useful – and appropriate – metaphor for understanding compact disc technology. We are all familiar with the vinyl recordings of music that, in past years, were the underpinnings of a huge worldwide leisure industry. The single, long spiral groove on a record carries in it mechanical wiggles that make a stylus tracking quickly through it vibrate. Gramophones work by spinning the plastic disc at a constant number of revolutions every minute while the stylus passes along the entire length of the groove. The vibrations in the stylus are converted into a tiny electrical signal which changes in intensity with the changes in the vibration. This rapidly varying signal is cleaned up, amplified and converted into audible sound via a speaker. In this way, the mechanical variations in the surface of the disc are preserved through a number of key stages. First, they are detected and converted into a sympathetically varying electrical current. Then the variations are amplified. Finally, they are turned back into mechanical variations in the form of oscillations in the air which we interpret as sound. Throughout, the information – whether a symphony by Beethoven or a gig by Blur – is being conveyed by a continuously varying quantity. In other words, the entire system is analogue.

In a compact disc, the information is coded in a similar way. A stylus runs through a spiral track and detects mechanical variations in it. But compact disc media need to carry a lot of information so we have to make two important modifications. First, we change the plane of the spiral track so that the mechanical fluctuation in it is vertical not horizontal. Second, we use a tiny laser as the stylus and use this to detect mechanical variations.

If you look at a compact disc you will be struck by the beautiful silvered appearance it shares with video disc. Like the video disc, its surface is covered by a highly reflective aluminium layer that allows a laser beam to bounce off its surface with practically no loss of intensity. What you cannot see easily with the naked eye is the single, tightly packed spiral track covering the surface. Typically, the spiral is packed to within 1.6 millionths of a metre of itself. If it was peeled off the disc and laid out in a straight line, it would measure nearly 3 miles in length.

If you looked at the track through a powerful microscope you would see the key to CD technology. Unlike a gramophone record, which has wiggles in the side of its track, here you would see variations in the floor. A series of minute pits are etched into the surface. In other words, if we imagine the track on a vinyl record as a meandering river whose banks wander from side to side, the compact disc's track is more like a steep and smooth-sided canyon with a bumpy floor along which the stylus hurtles.

A major advantage of using a stylus made of light is that it makes no physical contact with the surface of the disc. This means that neither the stylus nor the disc can ever wear out. Also, because a laser can be focused with pinpoint accuracy, it is possible to coat the surface of the disc with a tough, clear plastic. This protects the disc from dust and scratches while allowing the laser beam to penetrate and focus on the 'floor' of the information carrying track. As the beam sweeps along the floor it identifies the presence of the pits in the silvered substrate by the drop in reflectivity they cause. The fluctuations in the reflected laser beam are read at the head of the stylus as 'pit', 'no pit'. Two states: there or not there. On, off. Zero, one. In other words, binary code – the language of computers. So compact discs carry information in digital form, packed tightly in the single spiral track of a 12-centimetre diameter silver disc.

Unlike the video disc, what is being measured is not the length of the pits – the constantly varying value which gives video disc its analogue character – but merely whether or not a pit is there. This means the pits can be very small and a huge number can be carried in the 3 miles of track. In fact, translated into the measure of computer memory, a single compact disc can carry about 650 megabytes (65 million bytes) of information. Even today when magnetic hard disks are commonly offering hundreds of megabytes, this is a formidable amount of capacity. In 1985, when compact discs were first used to store computer data rather than digital music, a single megabyte of hard disk storage in a computer was substantial. So the 650 megabyte capacity of what became known as a compact disc 'read only memory' (CD-ROM) was nothing less than staggering. Even more striking than the sheer capacity was the low cost per byte of the medium. No other medium – either then or now – has even come close to the economy of optical storage. Depending on the numbers manufactured at one time, a compact disc can cost between about 50 pence and £1 sterling to produce. On this basis, each byte can cost as little as 0.00001 pence – orders of magnitude cheaper than solid state memory and vastly cheaper than any existing magnetic medium.

THE EVOLUTION OF CD-ROM MARKETS

When CD-ROM appeared in 1985, it was a solo initiative by Philips and Sony, the creators of the compact disc, backed extensively by the computer hardware industry which scented a new line of product development to exploit. Unlike its predecessor, the blockbuster entertainment medium, compact disc audio, CD-ROM was a medium firmly designed for computer users, requiring expensive new disk drives to be connected to desktop PCs to let users access the digital data stored on the discs. The step from CD-audio to CD-ROM had not been a simple one. Although in both cases, the information on the discs consists entirely of bits, in the case of CD-ROM the bits had to be stored in a specific and standard fashion so that all kinds of computers could get at the information. In other words, while CD-audio demanded a physical standardisation, CD-ROM required a deeper level of standardisation affecting the logical structure of the data on the discs. The process of agreeing the standardisation is an epic story in itself but it resolved itself when – in the late 1980s – the International Standards Organisation agreed a universal specification for all CD-ROM discs, designated as ISO 9660. From a publishing point of view, this was a crucial step because standardisation meant that all discs produced to ISO 9660 could be played on all CD-ROM drives manufactured to the same standard. Although, in the very early stages after the launch of CD-ROM, there were some maverick formats around, very quickly the industry settled into conformity and, to all intents, ISO 9660 became the defining specification for all forms of CD-ROM technology.

From the point of view of market development, however, the key factor was the rather arcane and isolated nature of early CD-ROM technology. It was overtly computeresque, demanding computer equipment for playback and computer expertise from its users to make sense of the processes of loading and running the disc and manipulating the search and retrieval software either embodied on the CD-ROM or supplied separately. Viewed from the present day, these characteristics of CD-ROM may not look particularly arcane or isolating. But in the mid-1980s, the personal computer was only just staggering to its feet as a pervasive and powerful new tool. Computers were expensive, unfriendly and largely unknown devices – except in those niches where access to electronic information was at least a partially established tradition. In other words, the original market for CD-ROM, and its commercial centre of gravity for many years afterwards, was those sectors in which computers were widely used and where electronic information was appreciated. This translates into professional information users – predominantly public and corporate librarians, academics and, slowly at first but gathering pace, managers in corporations with direct access to PCs.

This tight focus in terms of the users of CD-ROM did not mean there was any serious early volume in the market. David Worlock, now head of the London-based consultancy Electronic Publishing Services, recalls that he was one of the first British publishers to issue a CD-ROM title when in late 1985 he released a high priced CD-ROM database of legal information. He still reckons it was one of the boldest strokes in the history of publishing because, at the time, there were only about two CD-ROM drives in the UK – and one of those was on his desk! In other words, the early CD-ROM publishing industry suffered from a serious 'chicken and egg' problem. Publishers were reluctant to release titles because there were no CD-ROM drives in the hands of potential customers. Potential customers were reluctant to purchase drives because there were no titles to buy. It is not surprising, therefore, that one of the first CD-ROM directories, published as a thin, loose leaf folder by the London firm, TFPL, recorded only about 50 commercially available titles at the end of 1986. At that time, worldwide, the installed base of drives was about 6,500. At the end of 1994, by contrast, the same directory was a weighty tome with over 1,000 pages, printed on near bible paper to reduce bulk, containing details of around 8,000 titles. The worldwide base of drives, meanwhile, had grown to about 25 million.

As the 'chicken and egg' problem was gradually cracked by innovative, bold and both non-commercial and uncommercial publishers issuing CD-ROM titles in the teeth of a market of first a few hundred, then a few thousand drives, the initial commercial orientation remained fixed. The CD-ROM publishing industry addressed a market of desktop computer users. This meant professional, academic and – increasingly as the 1980s wore on – corporate users. The business model for this kind of publishing unsurprisingly followed the already well-established one familiar in online database markets. Very expensive products were sold to the few organisations who could afford to buy them. It was a high priced, low volume business with titles typically selling a few hundred copies at prices which varied from a few hundred to a few thousand pounds sterling. The products themselves were predominantly textual databases, often offcuts of some of the massive online databases that had been hosted for years on huge centralised computer systems and sold expensively via networks to small groups of academics and professionals with a strong 'need to have' motivation to pay the high cost of access.

Two basic pricing models emerged and are still commonplace for professional CD-ROM products. The simplest and most obvious is a straightforward one-off sale, usually – because of the market orientation – at very high price. More commonly, however, subscriptions are sold which give users access to a series of discs in the course of the year embodying monthly, quarterly or six-monthly updates of the underlying information. Clearly, the frequency of updates depends on how important the currency of the information is for users. Because of the technical and physical problems of creating updates on short timescales – except, of course, at extravagant premium prices – monthly updates are generally the most frequent. The idea of selling users 'access' in this pricing model is a key idea. Selling access means not selling the physical discs. In other words, all the customer purchases by paying a subscription is a licence which permits them – under certain stated conditions – to have access to the information stored on the discs. This is a vital point for publishers because it makes it easy for them to craft careful licence agreements to protect the valuable content of the discs from illicit use. A signature on such an agreement, and an unambiguous link between vendor and purchaser through such a licence contract, make it easier for publishers to enforce limitations on use and take sanctions against downright criminality. The most obvious dangers are resale of data, downloading and illegal copying, placing the CD-ROM on a network to enable large numbers of simultaneous users to benefit from the purchase of a single disc and – increasingly important as cheap, plug-and-play recordable CD-ROM systems become widely available – the illegal duplication of discs either for internal use by the purchaser's corporation or for straightforward commercial piracy. Subscription-based selling also ensures publishers get the outdated discs back from customers when a new version is issued. Early on, publishers found that if they did not do this a 'black market' trade rapidly emerged in 'old discs' resold by original purchasers at discounted prices to others who were less fussy about how up to date the products were.

While these pricing models ensure potential profitability and – through subscriptions – reasonable control over high-value content, the marketing of titles has the attraction of requiring no radically new strategies. Traditional, print-on-paper specialists, for example, with experience of publishing for defined vertical markets can simply apply their established marketing approach. The key – as ever – lies in knowing the market and reaching it as cost effectively as possible with suitable product information and pricing deals. As with all electronic product, of course, CD-ROM databases cannot be subjected to the 'flick test', beloved by purchasers of books and periodicals. To gain a sense of the value of a major CD-ROM title, potential purchasers usually need to use or sample it. This has the fairly obvious message, that publishers of these kinds of products must either arrange a try-before-you-buy system or provide a money-back guarantee of some kind. So, in addition to conventional direct marketing strategies commonplace in vertical market sectors, publishers commonly dispense sample discs and run 'satisfaction guaranteed' schemes. The other minor divergence from traditional marketing practices – although based on established models – is the use of specialist distributors who offer a wide range of products from different publishers via catalogue mailings and – in the case of high added value reselling – also run road-show-style demonstrations of product. The main headline for this genre of product, however, is that – with some obvious, minor exceptions – it is business as usual for vertical market publishers. The products may be silver discs rather than print-on-paper books or journals but selling them is not a lot different.

The more fundamental challenge is not marketing strategy but product design. Here, traditional publishers are at a serious disadvantage. There is a common assumption that publishers – especially specialist publishers – know their market-place. In a sense, of course, they do or they would not survive long. But publishing is not yet about understanding what people do with the information printed inside books. It is purely about trying to get as many people to buy the books in the first place. Now, to most outsiders, it would seem obvious that the two are connected. But the publishing industry has thrived on being good at packaging and marketing content while remaining ignorant of the detailed way in which their customers use – or may wish to use – the information and knowledge contained in the products. Publishers have a broad brush understanding that certain categories of people like books and periodicals on particular themes. But they are blissfully unaware of how much of what they publish is actually read, the detailed way in which information is utilised, shared or analysed by customers and what people do with the information when (and if) they access it. A book sale is a book sale. That is the only statistic a publisher cares about. If a book sells a lot of copies, it is successful and the publisher has shown flair. If it sells badly, the publisher has demonstrated bad judgement and an editor – probably – gets fired. The perfect example is Stephen Hawking's remarkable but largely impenetrable *A Brief History of Time*. It must be the only book to have sold in its millions because people wanted to possess the book rather than read it. The publishers, however, are far from concerned whether anyone was actually able to get beyond page 2 because – for whatever reason – the volume and rights sales were phenomenal. Understandably, this was the only arbiter of success that the publisher required. CD-ROM publishing for professional, corporate markets and academic markets is different – in spades.

Users of high priced CD-ROM titles do not want copies of discs to leave on coffee tables to impress guests. Neither do they buy them because they are fashionable or because they think that by physically owning the discs they possess the knowledge they contain. Instead, they buy discs because of specific, operational needs. And they are not merely seeking the raw information. The powerful appeal of CD-ROM in this market which makes it possible to sustain such high prices, is the power of the technology to offer rapid search and analysis features, added values that deliver high levels of benefit either because they save time or because they help users make more accurate decisions or both. This suggests two things. First, with such a high procedural element behind the customer's requirements, it is possible to draw up a clear, detailed blueprint for any particular product. In other words, publishers can literally define exactly what a customer needs and then design into the software on the CD-ROM an answer that addresses those needs. Second, while it is possible to blueprint products in principle, in practice it demands that publishers get to know their customers very well – something that they have been notably reluctant to do in the past. It is not surprising therefore that some of the most successful CD-ROM publishers for vertical markets have not come from the print-on-paper industry but from electronically based sectors such as online. There is a clear message here. For corporate, professional, academic markets – and in any form of electronic publishing aimed at such sectors – publishing success lies in defining the customers' needs and designing a functionality into the products that addresses them. It is as simple as that.

THE CONSUMER MARKET EMERGES

And it would have remained that simple if something quite unexpected had not have taken place in the early 1990s. With the benefit of hindsight, it should not have seemed so unexpected. After all, the market focus of CD-ROM had always been based on a simple logic. Access to CD-ROM titles demands elaborate computer hardware. So the market can exist only where such hardware is relatively commonplace. As we have seen, when CD-ROM first appeared in 1985, desktop computers were largely confined to informational professionals and academics. Not surprisingly, therefore, the first customers for CD-ROM technology were librarians and academic researchers. Within a few years – as computing became cheaper and marginally more friendly – PCs became increasingly common on the desks of business executives. This launched the corporate sector of the CD-ROM market-place. As computing became still cheaper and ever more accessible, it should have come as no surprise to see a market in homes emerging for consumer CD-ROM products. In fact, it seemed to come like a bolt from the blue. Suddenly, the Western world woke up to the fact that millions of powerful desktop computers were being purchased for use in homes. The PC was on its way to becoming a consumer appliance.

Perhaps one of the chief reasons why this came as such a shock to many observers was because a new generation of special CD-ROM appliances designed specifically for consumer use was supposed to be taking the ground that PCs were inheriting. The smokescreen created by the marketing hype surrounding them had taken a great many eyes off the ball.

To understand this important strand of development, we have to step back to the mid-1980s and the emergence of CD-ROM as an expensive, arcane, computeresque technology. Indeed, to distinguish it from the consumer appliances that followed, we will refer to CD-ROMs accessed by computers that look like computers as PC CD-ROM.

Even as Philips and Sony were releasing the first PC CD-ROM drives and the world was scratching its head and wondering what to do with them, a deeper, long-term strategy was already being formulated to bring CD-ROM into our living rooms. At the time, with only a few thousand drives in use anywhere in the world, it was an audacious concept. How could CD-ROM possibly be construed as a mass market medium when it was still struggling to be born as a highly technical, vertical market product? For Philips, however, the evolution of CD-ROM from its origins in CD-audio was part of a vital process of evolving a long-term commercialisation of the underlying technology. They had built CD-audio for the consumer market and after a slow start it had become the biggest consumer electronics success since the television. Then came CD-ROM, based on a consumer technology but reinterpreted as a professional information product. The next step was to reformulate CD-ROM and revisit the potentially lucrative consumer market. The path was therefore clear: an entertainment product was evolved into a professional product which in turn was to be evolved into an entertainment product again. Philips wanted to build a virtuous circle and make a small fortune by establishing CD technology as the most pervasive entertainment and information medium the world had ever seen – at least, since the creation of the printed page.

Philips' strategy for achieving this was based on one very good and one very bad idea. The very good idea was to create a computer capable of playing CD-ROM titles that was disguised to look like a domestic appliance, as easy to operate as an electric kettle. The very bad idea was to imagine that such an appliance would be used by a nuclear family to share a rich, interactive experience together in front of their television screen in the living room. The evolved form of CD-ROM which Philips developed is called compact disc interactive (CD-I). Physically, it is a neatly designed black box which racks well with the usual hi-fi and video paraphernalia in many living rooms. The fact that the box contains a combined multimedia computer and CD-ROM drive is cunningly disguised and the device is simply positioned as a multimedia entertainment appliance. From a marketing point of view, of course, that positioning is anything but simple, as Philips found early on when it tried to explain to an uncomprehending audience what 'interactivity' and 'multimedia' meant. In other words, while simple in concept, the process of communicating the product offering in terms the market could understand was a challenging – and as yet largely unsolved – problem, one that was to cripple the early take-up of CD-I players.

Because it is aimed at the living room, CD-I is designed to offer the kind of multimedia experience best suited to a living-room environment. In other words, CD-I's operating system (known as RTOS – real time operating system) is optimised to deliver a highly televisual form of multimedia best viewed from middle distance, rich with sound and images and capable of emulating the syntax of television-like programming. The hardware is designed, of course, to play back via a conventional domestic television while interaction with the software is governed not by a keyboard but by a simple, infra-red remote control device. Although a control of this kind limits the intensity of the interactivity, it perfectly suits the traditional approach to controlling television and other media experiences in the living room.

The history of CD-I's efforts in the consumer market is salutary. Other emulators such as Commodore with its CDTV system and 3DO with a consumer CD-ROM 'black box' technology boasting 'a quantum leap in graphics performance', all ran into the same brick wall. Although the detailed analysis is complex, the bottomline is simple. On the whole, consumers want to do two closely connected things in front of their television screen: relax and have fun. In other words, early CD-I titles – largely funded by Philips because few other content or development companies would risk investment in the new system – which aimed to provide rich, interactive cultural and educational experiences were simply barking up the wrong tree. Titles like *The Russia of the Czars* and *Treasures of the Smithsonian*, beautifully produced as they were, were too much hard work for the average consumers. And since software inevitably sells hardware, Philips rapidly found themselves unable to sell CD-I readily much beyond that eternal, mad band of early adopters who seem to buy any new consumer electronics technology that comes to market.

The acid reality of the market-place caused Philips to revamp its software development strategy and it is worth noting two things immediately. First, at the early stages of establishing any new consumer multimedia system it is ultimately software development strategy that determines the future of the related hardware. Consumers understand the hardware offering via the software. Which is just another way of saying that technology does not sell. What sells is the application of technology – what it can do for us and the benefits it can deliver in our lives. The second key point is that when a proprietary technology like CD-I is trying to establish an installed base, the hardware originators cannot shirk getting involved in shaping and driving the software strategy. The reason is self-evident. Few software developers or publishers are likely to be so utterly confident of a new platform that they will invest heavily in developing software for it without some cast-iron guarantees about the growth of an installed base of users – which is jargon for the emergence of a decent number of customers. No such guarantees can ever be given so, most times, the hardware companies have to bite the bullet and fund software development. Philips bit the bullet right through with CD-I and not only funded but also embraced software development as a new strategic strand in its core business. But recognising the realities of the market meant casting aside the former emphasis on worthy interactive titles and turning instead to mainstream entertainment. This meant two main themes: games and movies.

MULTIMEDIA ENTERTAINMENT IN THE HOME

Games was, in principle, a simple category to exploit because it belonged to a pre-existing genre. CD-I's problem in this sector was simply that the technology had not been optimised for game play. Other hardware makers with a tight specialism in games – such as Sega and Sony – both espoused CD-ROM 'black box' technology by creating new multimedia machines designed to squeeze the maximum games-playing potential from the systems. The result has been specialist CD-ROM players such as Sega's Saturn and Sony's Playstation which combine immense computing power with CD technology at incredibly low prices. As a result, the technology hits the high volume mainstream of the video games market while CD-I struggles in the shallows as 'a machine on which games can be played' rather than competing as a dedicated games console that can really deliver the business.

In the area of movies, CD-I is on firm ground and indeed Philips have been instrumental in creating a new sub-category of the CD-ROM standard known as VideoCD which plays – among other platforms – on CD-I. VideoCD is merely a flavour of CD-ROM that sacrifices interactivity for an ability to replay linear, full screen, full motion movies. In other words, because it has limited interactive features, comparable to the kind offered by CD-audio – the ability to shuffle and programme the playback of 'tracks' – it does not need to dip down into the operating system of its host machine. This means that so long as the host has the appropriate means of handling the video data built into its electronics, it can play VideoCD titles. VideoCD is, therefore, the first true cross-platform, multimedia CD format.

There are two levels at which taking this direction presented special problems and special advantages for Philips. The problems were both technological and commercial. At a technological level, creating a CD-ROM video standard meant being able to compress – in a universally standard way – the huge amount of digital information needed to represent a complete video so that it could be stored on a disc. Second, it meant making it possible for CD-I players to decompress this information so that the reconstructed video could be played back on a TV screen in real time. This was a big task. As we saw in chapter 2, a single frame of full screen TV quality video needs almost a whole megabyte of digital information to represent it fully. And to deceive the eye into thinking it is watching 'full motion', that frame has to be refreshed 25 times a second in Europe or 30 times a second in the United States (because, although eyes are much the same, television standards are not). In other words, on a European basis, about 20 megabytes of data every second need to be processed, transferred and displayed by the multimedia player in order for the screen to produce a full screen, full motion video experience.

If the multimedia is being delivered from a CD-ROM, the problem is complicated still further. Aside from the raw storage issue – and 650 megabytes of CD-ROM is soon consumed by uncompressed video information – there is an additional limitation in the underlying technology. CD-ROM is derived from its CD-audio forebear. CD-audio was optimised to give maximum linear play time rather than to allow interactivity and fast data transfer. This process of optimising the technology included a standard speed at which the disc was spun in the player. Because data on a CD can be read by the laser stylus only when the disc physically passes beneath the stylus, the speed at which the disc spins defines the rate at which the stylus can retrieve information from its surface. It turns out that for standard CD systems this rate of transfer is around 150 kilobytes per second. So, even if we stored 30 seconds of uncompressed video on a CD – which is about the most we could achieve – we could not retrieve it anything like fast enough to deliver full motion because we would need to take data from the disc at many times its maximum rate. One solution, of course, is to spin the disc faster and – as the CD-ROM market has matured – double and quadruple speed CD-ROM drives have emerged. But at the time this issue was first being resolved the 'speed of light' for drives was firmly 150 kilobytes per second and the implications of this ultimate limitation had to be addressed.

CD VIDEO

We have already discussed the process of compressing and decompressing digital video in some detail in chapter 2. But, to save us making awkward cross-references to that earlier material, we will reprise some of it in the particular context of CD media to see how such compression–decompression schemes are bringing video to the experience of multimedia CD-ROM.

The business of compressing data sufficiently to achieve at the least the storage part of the equation was well established and – by the early 1990s – already enshrined in an international technical standard called MPEG

(Motion Picture Experts Group – the name of the original team that figured the standard out). Its first phase standard is actually called MPEG-1. Uprated and more extreme compression schemes based on the same underlying mathematics are also now established. Most importantly of these, MPEG-2 is now about ready to begin delivering the first high density CD-ROM media and to transform digital data and television broadcasting.

This, however, addresses one part of the problem. Compressed digital signals or data can be fitted into less bandwidth – in the case of transmitted media – or squeezed onto less CD-ROM real estate in the case of offline, packaged media. But once compressed, the user still has to decompress it in order to view the original, reconstructed information. In other words, finding an effective way of compressing the data is only half the battle. If the means of compression, for example, requires users to have a Cray supercomputer to decompress the data, the scheme is plainly commercial nonsense. If it is to be useful, digital compression technology must also allow easy and cheap decompression by end users – otherwise it is like teaching a dog to dance on one leg: interesting, clever, but ultimately totally pointless.

As we implied earlier, MPEG compression is the real heavyweight contender among compression schemes, delivering excellent quality at an affordable encoding price. The level of performance it delivers, however, permits only 72 minutes of video per CD-ROM – so feature films have to be delivered in two or three disc sets – and the quality of playback is generally no better than VHS tape quality. However, it is an immediately available, 'good enough' solution. Its real drawback is less its overall performance than the grunt it requires of host computers in order to decompress the information it delivers. In practical terms, this means that to handle MPEG video, most of the desktop computers in use today need a power boost in the shape of a dedicated MPEG chip, designed to handle the decompression for the PC. The big advantage for the proprietary CD-ROM multimedia players – the so-called 'black boxes' – is that the chips needed to decompress MPEG video and other data can be included in the 'black box' itself – the razor can be sold with the razor blade. The hardware, after all, is dedicated to a particular purpose and it can generally be assumed that customers will want what is offered or else they would not buy it in the first place. In the case of CD-I, for example, VideoCD – which is designed around MPEG-1 compression – is an integral part of Philips' offering so building in an MPEG chipset and including it in the pricing of CD-I players makes obvious sense in terms of Philips' market proposition.

The situation, however, is completely different in the generic world of PC CD-ROM. Here different PC manufacturers provide a myriad of variations upon a hardware theme, each trying to make their computers distinctive at a competitive price for an increasingly discerning audience.

Most fundamentally, of course, PCs from any manufacturer are, almost by definition, general purpose devices. In other words, in functional terms, they lie at the opposite end of the spectrum from dedicated devices such as CD-I players and games consoles. PCs offer a range of possible functions driven by the wide range of applications software that can be run on them. It may well be that increasing numbers of PCs have more or less standardised multimedia capabilities built into them but we are a long way, for example, from being able to assume that PC users will routinely want to play VideoCD or, more generally, to access full screen, full motion video as a feature of interactive CD-ROM titles. This means something very simple in commercial terms. If people do not want it routinely, they should not routinely be made to pay for it as a part of the price of their hardware. It makes better sense to give purchasers the option of buying the PC without MPEG video chips inside and acquiring those chips as an upgrade if it turns out to be something they do want in future. Out of this simple idea has grown a massive spin-off business from the PC industry, solely concerned with creating and marketing upgrade kits, to deliver not only MPEG decompression but also a wide range of bolt-on functionalities for PCs.

For a combination of reasons, MPEG cards for PCs have not yet sold strongly although they are now widely available from a range of suppliers both in the United States and Europe. We are, of course, moving towards the time when MPEG will be cheap enough and compact enough to be included within PCs at very little additional cost. In much the same way as PCs are routinely being sold with built-in CD-ROM drives, therefore, we will soon find them coming equipped with MPEG video chips whether we are interested in video or not. Meantime, however, multimedia CD-ROM publishers have to address as wide a market as possible and cannot rely on customers having the necessary MPEG chips in their machines or being willing to make a special purchase and go through all the anguish of installing such chips, merely to view their latest CD-ROM title. In other words, publishers have to find a generic means of delivering video if they wish to include it at all. The most widely used solution is to dispense with MPEG schemes – which continue (largely and currently) to demand the decompression power of additional chipsets – and decompress the stream of digital video data using instead a much weaker system based not on special hardware but on a proprietary computer program designed specially for the purpose.

Meanwhile, VideoCD is now one of the main drivers of market demand for CD-I and deals by Philips acquiring VideoCD rights from major Hollywood studios have ensured a steady flow of high profile titles. Elsewhere independent publishers – particularly in Europe and Japan – have either turned their own video assets into VideoCD titles or acquired rights to enable them to issue VideoCDs based on other people's assets. The great attraction has been the low cost of encoding the video and, therefore, the commercial ease of transferring content from tape to disc, and the lure of a cross-platform format. The fact that the cross-platform nature of VideoCD has so far been a more theoretical than practical benefit has done little to stem the enthusiasm of the proponents of VideoCD and hundreds of titles are now available with many more in preparation.

THE DIGITAL VIDEO DISC

The enthusiasm for VideoCD, based as it is upon the original MPEG-1 standard, has been noticeably muted in the United States. While Europe and Japan embraced the standard as a 'here and now, good enough' solution, US hardware and software companies stood back, questioning whether a system based on MPEG-1 really offered the added values needed to create a CD-based video standard that could compete with the utility and installed base of conventional videotape. While VideoCD was plainly a 'here and now' technology – at least, so far as CD-I was concerned – was it 'good enough' to make a substantial market breakthrough? For US companies, therefore, the issue was whether MPEG-1 was really the right horse to back. Perhaps being geographically close to the home of the movie industry affected their thinking because it was certainly true that Hollywood regarded MPEG-1 as far from being the Nirvana of a replacement for videotape. As far as the studios were concerned, VideoCD rights were a useful source of additional income – particularly at the prices Philips has been prepared to pay – so long as the deals were for movies which had already been fully exploited in conventional video formats. In other words, with a few exceptions, the majors were prepared to play along with VideoCD so long as it carried no threat to its mainstream revenue sources – box office, video and TV.

But was there any alternative to VideoCD on the horizon? Was there even the prospect of another horse to back? Certainly, when Philips launched VideoCD in 1994, it resolutely faced down suggestions from the industry that MPEG-1 systems were merely using an interim technology. It backed VideoCD to the hilt because VideoCD was the short-term saviour of CD-I and needed to be promoted strongly as a consumer product for the long term. In reality, however, Philips, together with its CD-I partners, Sony, was already developing the real video format for the long term and, as expected, it was based on a combination of MPEG-2 decompression combined with a revised form of CD-ROM technology offering vastly greater storage capacity than the existing generation of CD-ROM systems.

Late in 1994, Philips and Sony found their hand forced by an unexpected move by an alliance of hardware and software companies led by Toshiba. Toshiba announced it was going to establish its own variety of high density

CD-ROM standard, apparently ahead of the system being worked on by Philips and Sony. Toshiba's concept appeared to be similar to the Philips/Sony format. It also used a double layer of recording media on the disc with a clever technology with a variable focus laser enabling the laser stylus to read both layers independently. However, it differed in suggesting that the discs should be double sided. Nobuyuki Idei, Sony Corporation's managing director, immediately issued a statement reaffirming Sony's commitment to the single-sided, double-layer, high density specification and saying that 'after careful evaluation and consideration with Philips, Sony has no plans to support the specifications proposed by an alliance of seven companies'. The gang of seven that Idei referred to was led and masterminded by Toshiba but included some powerful allies such as one-time CD-I ally Matsushita, media giant Time Warner, Hitachi, Pioneer, MCA and Thomson.

Idei's statement was effectively a declaration of a format war despite the fact that there were strong similarities between the two. Both were based on MPEG-2 encoding and relied on variable rates of transferring data from the disc to the player in order to optimise the length and quality of playback. Both were also based on offering double play options. In other words, the standard playback for both formats is about 140 minutes – sufficient for most feature movies – but a 'double up' option is available to create 280 minutes of playback. One of the major differences between the two systems was how they each offered this. In the case of Sony and Philips approach, a second information layer was to be bonded to and located above the initial, standard layer. Toshiba's strategy is also to use two information layers but to bond them back-to-back to create a double-sided system.

Sony's rejection was ostensibly based on its view of the comparative quality and manufacturing costs of the two formats. Sony (and by implication, Philips) claimed that its single-sided approach combined high quality playback (comparable with video disc) with ease and, therefore, economy of manufacture. It pointed out that the new format will need only minor modification to existing CD manufacturing equipment and that players will require only a single laser pickup to read both conventional and high density CD media. This last point was crucial because it explicitly indicated that the Sony/Philips standard would mean that players can be made backwardly compatible with existing CD-ROM and VideoCD titles.

Sony had certainly hitched their argument to the key issue. Despite Toshiba's strong backing, its double-sided approach suggested that mastering and pressing plants would have to re-tool with special lathes and replicators to handle the new discs. Players too were unlikely to be cheap. The actual price depended on the engineering approach but unless users were going to flip double-sided discs over themselves, players would need two optical pickups. Leaving aside the complexity of just making this work, MPEG-2 players with double optics were unlikely to be a consumer priced item in the foreseeable future despite Toshiba's bold claims about $500 price points by 1996.

What did all this mean for VideoCD – the existing linear video standard – and for the real future of high density linear and interactive CD-ROM developments? It is important to appreciate two important sub-texts to the public posturing by both camps.

The first derives directly from Hollywood. The major studios – hugely influential as the source of a rich flow of high value content – were taking a big interest in the future of digital video. As we noted, earlier, apart from some careful deal-making over VideoCD rights, Hollywood was still waiting for a replacement for its cash cow, videotape, that would offer some distinctive added values. As far as it was concerned, VideoCD, with all the limitations of MPEG, was not it. Hollywood did not like the quality and it liked even less the maximum 72 minutes playing time which meant movies had to be delivered on multidisc sets. In fact, Hollywood had a very clear shopping list of features it was looking for in any new system. Discs must have enough play time to carry a complete feature film. This meant enough capacity to store at least 140 minutes of video, preferably much more. The playback quality had to be far superior to VHS. Ideally it should be comparable to the broadcast quality and stereo sound offered by analogue videodiscs and should also allow multiple soundtracks for dubbing purposes. The hardware and software would need to be parent friendly so a lock to provide unauthorised playback by children was essential. And, finally, the system must embody a foolproof anti-piracy device.

This was Hollywood's ideal shopping list – or, at least, the main items from it – and whether or not it could possibly get all that it wanted was less important than the power and strength of its lobby. By taking a public and prescriptive stand, the movie industry was effectively shaping the future of high density CD-ROM formats as a medium to play back movies. Not surprisingly, therefore, the format soon stopped being called high or super density and took on the generic title DVD, standing for digital video disc. This implied that interactivity was consigned firmly to the back seat. The use of high density for video-rich interactive applications in education, information and entertainment was purely secondary to creating a medium for playing back linear movies.

The second sub-text concerned control of patents. Seen from outside the scrum, the obdurate positions of Toshiba and its allies on the one hand, and Philips and Sony on the other, looked like an exercise of crass obstinacy. After all, a format war would benefit no one and the difference between the two technological solutions was really not great. Despite the high-minded talk about which system was 'superior' the real issue behind the spat was hardly discussed. The war was not a phoney one despite the fineness of the differences between the two sides. And neither was it a war – as it appeared to be – about formats. The real struggle was for the control of patents. Philips and Sony together were the creators of compact disc technology. As its creators, they also became proprietors of a number of key underlying patents which – translated into manufacturing licences – generate for both corporations huge sums in royalties from hardware manufacturers and disc replicators. For every CD audio or CD-ROM device made and for every disc pressed, Philips and Sony receive a payback. The development of ever more pervasive CD-based standards, therefore, was much more than a way of growing the opportunities for Philips and Sony to sell more of its own products. It was a way of selling more of everybody else's products too and so sustain and build their royalty cash flows. The battle by Toshiba to establish a new high density standard, therefore, was more than a threat to take a lead in the manufacture of its own VideoCD products. It was a threat to Philips' and Sony's continuing control of underlying patents and to the revenues that such patents guarantee.

In the middle of a long hot August 1995, in Europe, Philips finally came up with a compromise aimed at defusing the conflict and avoiding a costly and pointless battle in the market-place. At the time of writing, it is still too early to determine who has won and lost in this battle for control of the next major stage in CD-ROM evolution but it appears there has been give and take on both sides. The differences between the Toshiba-led Super Density Alliance and the Philips-Sony initiative had been getting more subtle as the months had passed but the final resolution appears to lean more towards Toshiba than Philips. A double-layer disc technology is going to be used – as first proposed by Toshiba – but both layers will be read from one side, as suggested by Philips and Sony. The outcome is a two-pronged standard offering backward compatibility with existing conventional density formats. There will be a single-sided, single-layer disc format providing a storage capacity of 4.7 gigabytes (a gigabyte is a thousand megabytes and the high density figure compares with 0.6 gigabytes currently offered by standard CD-ROMs). Using MPEG-2 compression, this will make it possible to accommodate all but the very longest feature movies on a single disc at a quality comparable to today's videodiscs. There will also be an ultra high density format using double-layering to give 8.5 gigabytes of storage. This is likely to be used for major, video-rich interactive applications. The first titles conforming to the new standards will be released with the first tranche of DVD players late in 1996 or early in 1997. There are as yet no public plans for interactive titles using the high density formats and few expect them to emerge until late 1997 at the earliest.

Even if the technological issues appear to have been resolved, however, a continuing source of concern for Philips and Sony is whether it can continue to claim ownership of underlying CD standards. In other words, even if the format war is over, the patent war may only just be beginning.

USING VIDEO IN CD MEDIA

Although there seems little to stop rapid progress in the development of powerful video technologies for CD media, it is worth pausing to consider just how important high quality, full screen, full motion video is in the first place. As with most things in publishing and media distribution, the heart of the issue lies in the notion of fitness of purpose. In other words, the needs of the market are paramount and products must be designed with those needs firmly in mind. For example, it hardly requires saying that the best quality, full screen, full motion video is essential if the CD product is designed to deliver a filmgoing experience. If the product is a movie – or a music video, which is a special case of the same thing – nothing else will do. Indeed, as we have already argued, the real driver behind the next generation of high density CD media is Hollywood and the search by studio moguls and others for an added value replacement medium for videotapes. The hugely increased storage capacity will eventually also be utilised for interactive products – especially video-rich ones – but the movie industry is first in line.

In edutainment, infotainment and games, however, the value of using full screen video of any kind is more arguable. The games industry right now is embracing CD video – at least, video decompressed in software so that it is played back in a smallish window – but it has special reasons for doing so. The cash cow of that industry – solid state cartridge games with the advantage of speed but the drawback of limited storage capacity – is in rapid decline. Most of the major console manufacturers are now moving their technologies increasingly towards CD-ROM based hardware. Nintendo is the major exception but even though it believes it has a super-magnetic disc technology up its sleeve, it is likely to fall into line with the rest of the industry in the long term. They are doing this both because CD-ROM is – for whatever reason – an attractive new product for games players and because they can use CD-ROM's capacity to deliver bigger games with more and better sound and graphics. The major problem which such manufacturers and their associated communities of software publishers have to address, however, is the slowness of the CD-ROM in delivering interactive experiences.

This relative slowness – especially compared to the lightning speed of cartridges – is due to the fact that CD-ROM drives have to physically move a stylus back and forth across the surface of a disc in order to locate and retrieve data. This mechanical process takes time and although careful design of where the data on the disc are placed and use of a modern PC's ability to hold large amounts of data in local buffers in its on-board memory, can disguise the limitation to a degree, games have to rely on much more than sheer speed of action to succeed. This has led games developers towards new genres of titles based more on cerebral values than the purely visceral appeal of fast action arcade games. The most obvious of these is the unfortunately named 'interactive movie'. This genre consists largely of traditional strategy games – with a leavening of arcade action – peppered with sequences of linear video in windows on the screen. When the video starts playing, however, the title stops being interactive. When the title stops being interactive, the experience of using it is fractured. In other words, instead of the video used this way becoming a cohesive and compelling feature within a CD-ROM title, it often fragments and ultimately undermines the experience of using it.

This highlights a key fact concerning digital video – currently it is a largely non-interactive ingredient in the interactive multimedia mix. Making it fully interactive, however, requires vastly more powerful technology than we can currently harness commercially. However, the immediate future looks promising not because linear video will be used any more wisely in interactive offerings but because a fully interactive alternative is in the wings. The next major move in uprating PC performance will come not via the wider use of MPEG video cards but through the emergence of accelerators that will allow ordinary PCs to handle 3D graphics and manipulate them in real time. This development – already partially visible among the most powerful games consoles – will turn PCs into virtual reality engines capable of delivering fully manipulable 3D experiences. In gameplay, this will mean that users will have complete control over their physical viewpoint and, more important, will have complete freedom to interact on a moment-by-moment basis with photorealistic 3D images. This, of course, is where the new role of video lies. Photorealism will partly come from the sophistication and resolution of the 3D images themselves but it will also increasingly spring from the ability to layer the images with video. This process – known as surface texturing – is already being used to add realism to 3D worlds. When we are able to texture with high quality video, the result will be breathtaking. It will also signal the end of the current generation of pseudo-interactive movies and the emergence of the real thing. Using video-textured, real-time 3D, users will be able to manipulate what appear to be normal video sequences. In reality, every element in each sequence will be computer generated with a video overlay texturing the graphics and, because of this, will be individually and independently manipulable by the user. The potential for immersing users in convincing 3D worlds will at last be available from ordinary desktop technology.

What about the role of video in information and education? Here the argument for full screen, full motion video is much weaker and the need for high levels of interactive 3D graphics is less obvious. Indeed, in even the best multimedia edutainment and infotainment products, the inclusion of full screen video segments would be a serious interruption to the flow of the title and add nothing worth having to the experience of using it. In other words, judiciously selected and well-implemented partial-screen video – even if it is of modest quality – is a good enough enrichment of underlying content. Why try to offer more? Indeed, the rule that emerges from these considerations suggests that where video is an enrichment rather than the central focus of a product, windowed video is not merely adequate but wholly appropriate. Where video is the central focus, full screen delivery is plainly important. However, the overriding issue is even more basic. Ultimately, the commercial success of the consumer CD-ROM market rests on how well the video is synthesised along with all the other elements of multimedia content to produce a product that satisfies its market.

THE DISTRIBUTION NIGHTMARE

As this book is written, a growing realisation is dawning that the consumer CD-ROM market is heading towards considerable crisis. There is a heavy irony in this because the awareness of impending disaster is emerging just as the market appears to be rocketing in size. The statistics – albeit US ones – speak for themselves. At the end of 1993, the US market generated by sales through direct and retail channels and bundled OEM (original equipment manufacturer) deals between publishers and hardware vendors, was worth about $200 million. A year later, the market had topped $650 million. By the end of 1995 it had touched $1.5 billion. Apart from the sheer pace and magnitude of the growth, there are two very important factors hidden in the statistics.

First, the number of units reaching the market through sales to consumers now vastly outstrips the number being given away free as titles bundled with hardware purchases. In 1995, such bundles represented about 35 per cent of all units reaching the US market. Two years earlier, the figure had been around 70 per cent. This is highly significant because it appears to indicate a crucial underlying trend. Instead of getting CD-ROM titles free with hardware, consumers are purchasing titles themselves, presumably because of a specific, strong interest in them. In other words, market demand has arrived and instead of title publishers pushing their titles at consumers through giveaways, they are beginning to feel the welcome effect of consumers coming in off the street keen at last to buy their products.

Second, although the figure has declined somewhat since 1993, around 40 per cent of the sales are generated by content-based titles. In other words, info- and edutainment is a large sector of the market with games a comparable but by no means dominant category. This is good news for the mainstream publishing community unfamiliar with games industry culture and – coupled with spectacular market growth – has played an important part in the rapid expansion in the number of titles being issued. In 1994, for example, as the market more than trebled in size within a single year, developers and publishers rushed to meet the rising tide of demand with a vast number of new titles. At the end of 1993, fewer than 400 CD-ROM titles with true consumer market orientation were available worldwide. Twelve months later the number had swollen to around 3,000. Since then, not only has the raw number of titles continued to increase but also development budgets have soared as publishers have struggled to distinguish their offerings with ever more spectacular visual effects, ever more tightly packed content and ever more big name film actors to 'star' in their productions.

But market growth, and the publishing frenzy it provoked, seems to contain the seeds of its own destruction. The avalanche of new titles has created a massive log jam in retail distribution channels. Shelf space is at a premium. In the United States, where the market is most advanced, even the most committed CD-ROM retailers are stocking only 300–400 titles and, from retailer to retailer, they tend to be the same 300–400 titles. In other words, the vast majority of new products are failing to get retail exposure. None of this is surprising. The market-place has simply expanded faster than the retail infrastructure for handling it. This is not the contradiction in terms it seems, simply because it is not retail distribution alone that is permitting market growth. Bundling – despite the decline in its influence – and direct distribution are both still major components. But the slow growth of retail support is a major inhibitor and a serious problem for publishers and developers alike.

EUROPEAN MARKETS EMERGE

Virtually everything we have stated so far about the consumer market has related to events in the United States and for good reason. The shift in the centre of gravity of PC CD-ROM publishing first emerged most emphatically and obviously in the United States and while the US market differs substantially in structure, culture and metabolism from Europe, it is nonetheless a useful laboratory for studying the underlying processes of change soon to sweep through European markets. To get a sense of just how emphatic the shift in the States was, consider the proportion of the total PC CD-ROM population that was in US homes in the early 1990s. In 1991, a mere 4 per cent of all drives were in homes. By the end of 1993, the number had leapt to 60 per cent and reached 70 per cent a year later.

In Europe, the same pattern began to emerge in 1994. This was the year when the consumer PC CD-ROM market arrived – at least in terms of the numbers of CD-ROM drives in European homes. In 1993, for example, about 80,000 UK homes had PC CD-ROM drives. At the end of 1994, the installed base had soared to 500,000 and at the end of 1995 stood at around 1.7 million – a twenty times increase in two years! In Germany, the picture was even more dramatic: 127,000 drives rising to 1.1 million at the end of 1994 and jumping again to 3.1 million at the end of 1995. The pattern in France was 87,000 rising to 400,000 and then to 1.4 million at the end of 1995. This colossal growth, however, disguised a key factor in the metabolism of the market. While hardware purchases soared, CD-ROM software sales remained modest and patchy.

In particular, it was evident that the possession of CD-ROM drives no longer implied their use. In 1995 in the hottest European market, Germany, for example, 38 per cent of all CD-ROM homes possessed no discs at all. In France the figure was 13 per cent and in the UK 15 per cent. This apparently extraordinary finding has a simple explanation. As PCs increasingly have CD-ROM drives routinely built-in, buyers of PCs are getting hold of drives without being primarily interested in using them. Their principal motivation is to own a PC. This is radically different from the position only a few months previously when drives were purchased as a deliberate act, driven by real and specific interest in CD-ROM. The reason why the German percentage is so high is because in the German PC market aggressive hardware vendors such as Vorbis and Escom have made special efforts to bundle cheap CD-ROM drives with PCs to create ultra low cost, multifeatured packages.

All this says one very clear thing about any analysis of the European and, by implication, US markets. The link between the installed base of drives and a title market is weakening. The possession of the technology no longer implies its use. For Europe, in particular, this means that the huge rise in the drive population should not be taken to imply automatically a comparably large emerging title market. Indeed, in 1995, the realities were bleak for European multimedia publishers. In the UK, an average good selling edutainment or infotainment title was selling around 5,000 copies. One or two bestsellers were reaching about 20,000. In Germany, the country with by far the biggest and fastest growing population of CD-ROM drives, the picture was little different. Of around 1,700 titles available in German (both indigenous German language titles and English language imports), only 4 per cent sold more than 20,000 copies. About 6 per cent sold between 10,000 and 20,000 and 13 per cent between 5,000 and 10,000. This left over 75 per cent of titles selling 5,000 copies or fewer.

The real problem that these numbers imply is that the economics of selling fully featured CD-ROM titles into individual national markets does not work. The average levels of sale quoted above do not even allow publishers to recover their direct costs of production, let alone overheads. There is an exception, of course. The economics do not work but they do not work for indigenous European publishers. They can work for US companies who have already amortised most of their costs over domestic sales of their titles. For them, the European market is an excellent opportunity to escape the congestion of US distribution channels and the grief it is causing and mop up profit in Europe. The fact that this is taking place is indicated for all to see by export figures for the US consumer industry as a whole. In 1994, 24 per cent of the value of the US market was generated by export sales – mainly to Europe. Up to the mid-year of 1995, the figure had leapt to nearly 40 per cent. And in 1994, the 24 per cent was of a market of around $650 million. In 1995, assuming the percentage persisted to the year end, the 40 per cent was a substantial slice of a cake probably worth around $1.6 billion. It is no coincidence that in 1995 Encarta was the only information CD-ROM to feature in the top twenty bestsellers in the UK alongside of a wealth of games titles. Encarta, in fifth place, was a bestseller because it was for the first time localised to its market. The UK, for the first time, had a UK edition. This is an important straw in the wind. Not only are US publishers increasingly exploiting the European market, they are also taking it seriously. In other words, they are not merely seeking to shift a few additional units. They are investing in localising and reculturing their products in order to leverage them across the diversity of European national requirements and tastes.

This is strong medicine for European publishers. Already faced with a fragmented market, unviably low unit sales – except for a few hits – and an embryonic and diffident distribution infrastructure, they are in danger of being swept away by the big battalions from the United States. The only credible answer is for European publishers to rapidly develop pan-European strategies. This means a range of partnerships and alliances aimed at cross-leveraging titles with appropriate levels of sensitive localisation and reculturing. The European multimedia industries must work together in a realistic fusion of co-operation and competition in order to maintain a grip on the future of their own market-place. The UK publisher, Dorling Kindersley, has already demonstrated how well co-publishing models can work in the multimedia business and it is now increasingly important for others to follow its brilliant lead.

DEVELOPMENTS IN DISTRIBUTION CHANNELS

To gain an impression of how much further retail support still has to go before a really effective infrastructure is available, we only have to look at the estimated penetration of multimedia in the key retail sectors. Late in 1994, Richard Bowers, the Executive Director of the US Optical Publishers Association, published results of a study carried out in the previous summer. He found that the real focus of retail distribution remained in the specialist software stores. Out of 5,300 such stores in the United States about 4,500 were stocking multimedia CD-ROM titles. This is a penetration of 85 per cent. Elsewhere the picture, though fast evolving, was more patchy. Out of 16,500 computer and consumer electronic stores, for example, 2,000 (12.2 per cent) were stocking CD-ROM titles. Bookstores were beginning to emerge as a new and important sector. Out of 11,000 nationwide, around 500 (4.5 per cent) had made a commitment to CD-ROM but many others were planning to enter the market before Christmas. Bowers believed that bookstores would be the biggest single growth sector of 1995. Video stores were also expected to rapidly expand their involvement in multimedia, with Blockbuster leading the way with its formidable 4,000 store network. In the area of department stores, the plans of the major chains are crucial. In 1994, Bowers found, fewer than 500 such stores out of over 10,000 were stocking CD-ROMs. The turn-around in this sector – when it occurs – will have a huge impact because of the high volumes that such chains can achieve deploying their very high profile shelf space.

Even the anticipated growth in book and video retailers and department store chains stocking titles – a process which is taking much longer to develop than Bowers had thought in 1994 – is unlikely to bring much immediate relief to the immense congestion in US distribution channels. Indeed, whatever relief does emerge may come too late for many developers depending on cash flow from sales of titles they have joint ventured with larger content companies. Flush with recent injections of venture capital from bankers and financiers with a simplistic and rosy-eyed view of the growth of the consumer market, these small outfits have been at the forefront of the surge in new titles. They are now becoming the first to feel the backlash of the distribution crisis. The fully featured, big budget titles they have created need to find high volume outlets to recoup their investments on any reasonable timescale and, despite the significance of direct selling and bundling, serious volume can best be achieved through high street exposure.

The problems in getting shelf space most obviously hit small players with small lists or even just a single title to their name. But the majors are also feeling the pressure. Microsoft, for example, with all its power in the market-place and a large number of titles available in its Home brand series, is finding that it can gain consistent retail distribution only for a handful of its perennial bestsellers. Elsewhere, affiliate label programmes are also under pressure with organisations like Comptons New Media, Time Warner Interactive and Mindscape all having real difficulty in getting the full range of the titles in their care into the market. A serious commercial squeeze is being made even more dangerous by a rampant drive to cut street prices – at least, in the US market. In 1995, Microsoft, for example, slashed US prices of all its titles by an average of around 30 per cent. Publishers of mainstream encyclopedias such as Grolier, Comptons and Microsoft have seen their prices slip from around $200 in 1994 to under

$50 by late 1995. Elsewhere, specialist publishers such as Softkey have established new ground with budget edu- and infotainment titles, priced at under $20. The intent behind the downward spiral in pricing is clear. The hunt is on for shelf space and with it the ultra-high volumes of sale that will compensate for the crumbling price points. But results so far suggest that drastic price cutting is demolishing fragile margins rather than delivering the broadly based competitive advantage being sought. Falling prices may look good for consumers but, through their savage impact on margins, are threatening to destroy the underlying publishing industry. Price cutting alone, of course, is not the key issue. The real problem is price cutting products that have to fight their way through a pressurised value chain where distributors, sub-distributors and retailers all expect to take deep discounts out of the revenue stream. The price wars being fought in the United States have not yet fully impacted on the less well developed European market. But they will. Imported products from the States are already falling in price and while exporters will try to price to the higher levels acceptable to Europeans, the downward slide is inevitable. Where the imported products go, indigenous products must surely follow.

EVADING THE LOG JAM

As a result of these increasing difficulties, many publishers are examining new ways of reaching the market. Clearly, direct mail remains a key alternative but works best when purchasers already know what they want to buy. In other words, it is most effective when publishers can support direct mail with a concerted marketing and publicity campaign to raise awareness and interest in the title.

While direct mail remains an important avenue, however, a new distribution model is being tested which cuts out the problems of getting retail shelf space while, at the same time, giving purchasers a 'try before you buy' option. The new approach is based on the use of encryption techniques to 'cripple' access to the content of a CD title. The first consumer market example – aside from some home shopping initiatives based on CD-ROM 'catalogues' – was a title distributed in 1994 by Comptons and developed by Graphix Zone. The title had been created on behalf of the production company owned by pop star Prince (now renamed an unpronounceable symbol but for our non-hip purposes still referred to as 'Prince'). The title was ostensibly a new audio single called 'Prince Interactive' but the packaging invited purchasers who had CD-ROM drives to insert the discs into those drives in order to enjoy a special bonus. When they did so, Prince fans were presented with a playable demonstration of a Prince Interactive game featuring Prince music and video clips. In order to purchase access to the full game, the users were invited to call Comptons New Media and pay about $40 for a unique electronic key that would release the complete game. In other words, the original CD purchased in record stores for between $6 and $8 contained an open audio 'front end' to a much more expensive but electronically crippled multimedia product. Consider, however, what has occurred as far as the retailer is concerned. The retailer has sold a product for a few dollars and gained a margin based on that price. The publisher has distributed a high price product at a low price discount and gained a revenue stream free of deep dealer discounts. Equally important, the publisher is also put in direct contact with purchasers allowing the creation of a valuable proprietary consumer database for selling upgrades and new products.

The same underlying technique has also been used in an even more radical way. In the UK in December 1994, an issue of *PC Power* – one of the growing range of consumer PC magazines flooding the market – appeared with a CD-ROM mounted on its front cover. In itself, this was nothing exceptional. Such magazines are increasingly appearing with free, cover-mounted CD-ROMs. In this case, however, the CD-ROM contained a complete game – a high profile title from Infogrammes called 'Alone in the Dark'. The CD was described as a 'Play Before You Buy Edition' and purchasers of the magazines could play a part of the game on their multimedia personal computers (MPCs) before being presented – presumably at a suitably cliff-hanging moment – with a message telling them that if they wanted more they should call Infogrammes and purchase for £29.95 a code that would unlock the complete game.

Taken on their own, the Prince disc and the Infogrammes initiative look like isolated experiments. However, given the context of a major crisis in CD-ROM distribution in the United States and, as yet, the virtual absence of serious retail commitment in the UK, the use of crippling technology may become an important and influential new distribution model. Indeed, the Infogrammes example could be a watershed in the distribution of packaged media products and for two major reasons. First, we have hitherto always relied on a fixed pricing model based on a price defined at the moment and point of sale. By using crippling technology we can instead price at whatever level we like, whenever we like. If it had chosen, Infogrammes could have varied the price charged for the access code to the game on a daily or even moment-to-moment basis. Second, crippling fractures the link between the retailer and the retail price. In the case of the cover-mounted giveaway, of course, the retailer gives shelf space to a magazine which itself distributes a high priced media product. The Prince disc is an example of low price 'open' media products sheltering high priced but encrypted ones. The implication is serious for retailers who will have to find new ways to respond to this complex new ingredient in the distribution mix.

The complexity of the situation is likely to increase as encryption is used more creatively. It is possible for a variety of new, flexible pricing models to be applied by publishers. Encrypted CD titles, for example, can be priced on the basis of giving purchasers a fixed number of plays, unlimited plays for a limited time (with more time purchasable for additional cost), or selective access to different levels or dimensions of a product depending on the price paid. It is anyone's guess how these possibilities will eventually be commercialised but it is likely that we will see increasing experimentation during the coming years. One thing is certain, new pricing and distribution models will create major new pressures for deal-making among publishers, retailers and those – such as magazine proprietors – who can readily inject large numbers of encrypted discs into the market in some fairly targeted way. And the new deal structures will have to be founded on the back of new systems of auditing sales in order to make sure everyone appropriate can track the revenue streams in which they may have some percentage interest.

CD-ROM's END GAME

Increasingly, the multimedia CD-ROM industry is suffering serious commercial pain and some battered developers and publishers are beginning to question the unquestionable. Despite all the hype and hope of recent years, does consumer CD-ROM publishing have a long-term future? It has been an unquestioned article of faith in the CD media industry that the consumer market needs only an installed base of technology before it lifts off in spectacular fashion to create a rich, diverse and profitable title publishing market. But this idea emerged in those halcyon days when surfing was a watersport, nets were used for fishing and getting wired was a problem your electrician sorted out. Today's electronic media market is dramatically different. Instead of a landscape dominated by familiar, offline packaged media like CD-ROM, we now have complex play-offs between offline and online media and a burgeoning market for selling new forms of content and services over global networks. Even offline's much lauded ability to handle high quality interactive multimedia is looking increasingly unconvincing as a unique proposition as even narrowband networks – the kind that rely on nothing more space age than a telephone line – become capable of delivering 'good enough' multimedia to an expanding population of wired consumers.

Meantime, out on the battlefields, blood is being shed in pursuit of the original dream. The developers, publishers and distributors of multimedia are struggling up and down the value chain to bring an ever larger volume of CD-ROM titles to a growing number of users with CD-ROM drives attached to or built into their PCs. But as we have already noted, possession of the hardware, however, does not necessarily imply its use. This is a key idea which should be engraved on the hearts of everyone trying to commercialise this market. Most vividly, in Europe – where hardware bases are rising exponentially – title sales remain patchy and generally unexciting. In the United States – where hardware figures are equally spectacular – sales volumes are coming but only in a sharply polarised fashion. About 10 per cent of the titles are generating 80 per cent of the revenues and the vast majority are unprofitable for everyone except the retailers. Which 10 per cent is making the running? Inevitably, that small proportion of the available titles able to gain some scarce and expensive shelf space at retail. In other words, gridlock in US distribution channels is making those consumers that want CD-ROM see only the tip of a publishing iceberg. Multimedia CD-ROM is increasingly expressing itself as a hit-driven business with little range in its offerings. While this obviously appeals to some consumers – after all, someone is buying nearly $2 billion worth of discs – it certainly lacks the depth of appeal needed to stir a deeply rooted, long-term publishing market.

Failures and difficulties of some leading developers – Amazing Media and Mammoth Microproductions in the United States and Attica and MDI in the UK – are early signs of growing commercial pressure in the value chain. It is most visible among the originators of multimedia titles because this community consists mainly of small, financially fragile organisations. But, be sure, the pain is already spreading up the chain and we will see once-committed, enthusiastic publishers soon retrenching and looking elsewhere for more stable and profitable sources of electronic publishing revenues.

This does not mean that the consumer CD-ROM market is on the brink of failure. Far from it. But it tells us that the market will not be the one we have long expected. Instead, it will resolve itself into a fast and furious hit-driven environment majoring on games and mainstream entertainment – including, within two to three years, a strong market for largely linear digital video disc (DVD) offerings, including a wide range of the world's most popular feature films and music videos. Reference and information will play a part but success will be limited to a few major titles which will dominate the market. For those still wanting to play in this business, therefore, the only available strategy is to cultivate niches and colonise them as quickly as possible before competitors move in and take the same, limited turf. A key area in which niches abound is education and focused, special interest publishing. So the message for the consumer market is not that it is doomed but that our original vision of it was naïve and misplaced. To make money and prosper in the hard reality of the market-place we need either to make some big throws of the dice or take a more cunning view of the opportunities and become a shrewd, niche player.

Meantime, of course, a new form of publishing is emerging which increasingly merges offline and online media. We will examine online media in detail in following chapters but – even if it means readers looking ahead to clarify some of the terminology and concepts – it is worth mentioning right away the prospect of a powerful merger between offline and online publishing. As an infrastructure of network services unfolds, the possibility of embedding links to online sites within CD-ROM products looks increasingly plausible. The move to hybridise CD-ROMs in this way is already gathering pace rapidly in both the United States – where it is already an established publishing model – and, more slowly, in Europe, where a lack of consumer online services has so far held back commercial development.

The process of hybridising CD-ROMs offers major benefits for both publishers and customers. For customers, online links can enrich a CD-ROM title by providing access to additional information or even whole new tranches of product. A game – such as the bestselling *Myst* – can be sold as a fixed offline product and then updated over a network by downloading new chapters of the game to be stored on the user's hard disk and played using the software on-board the CD-ROM. Updates can also take the form of access to highly volatile information. Microsoft's 'Complete Baseball' – probably the first consumer hybrid – was aimed to provide a multimedia experience of baseball on the CD-ROM and access to latest sports results and news via a daily online link. Microsoft's latest audio counterpart of the bestselling *Cinemania*, a title called *Music Central*, allows you to go online and order the music titles you sample in the CD-ROM. New dimensions are also being added to information and reference products. Grolier Interactive's 1996 edition of its evergreen *Multimedia Encyclopedia* now contains hundreds of links to sites on the CompuServe network where its users can gain additional, related information or participate in forum discussions with other users with similar interests, exploring the same product.

The idea of communications of this kind is a powerful one – particularly since using a CD-ROM has traditionally been an inherently isolated (and, possibly, isolating) experience. Clearly, communication between publisher and customer via the hybrid links is a crucial means of building a relationship with the customer which can later be commercialised with new product and service offerings. But the same process of communication can just as easily take place amongst the users of the hybrid links themselves. In other words, hybrid CD-ROMs make it possible for publishers to build and manage communities of interest centred on their offline products but flourishing in the online environments. Such communities not only sustain but also spread interest in the offline product, strengthening sales potential, extending shelf life and enhancing the prospect of sequel or related new products.

Despite the rhetoric of some commentators, hybridising CD-ROMs is not a sign of the predicted decline of CD-ROM media in favour of online products and services, a kind of halfway house en route to an entirely wired future. Much more important than that – it is a good, common-sense publishing model that works if applied with careful regard to its inherent technical and creative challenges and can be deployed to maximise profit and commercial advantage in a tough market-place which will do nothing but get tougher.

But the CD-ROM market is a coat of many colours and while the consumer market – in spite of all its difficulties – hogs the industry headline, the less glamorous but also less tormented professional, corporate and academic market sectors continue to grow and to offer serious publishing opportunities. An obvious reason why these sectors are more readily commercialised is that they do not lean so heavily on such an inefficient distribution infrastructure as retail. Instead, they rely largely on well-established direct marketing and direct selling models which publishers can more or less transfer from their traditional business experience. From a content development point of view, the markets are grounded, refreshingly, in defined and definable customer needs which can be turned by the publisher into the distinct added value features which ultimately sell the products. If such products fail to sell, it is more than bad luck or the injustice of an immature distribution system. It is bad publishing.

However, even in these well-established sectors, the outlook is troubled. Although the causes may be different, the low volume, high price market may be in as much long-term trouble as the high volume, low price one. Corporate, professional and academic information users are increasingly drifting towards the use of the new generation of low cost networks where range of choice, keen pricing and new product features are making online information sources more attractive than ever before. Long before an online consumer market is generating significant global revenues, professional, business-to-business and intra-business markets will have migrated online – not into the vastly expensive and unfriendly clutches of the online database industry of yesterday but to a welcoming, cost effective and increasingly Internet-based environment. Good news for users but bad for those publishers wedded to a future of CD-ROM publishing.

All of which demonstrates how important it has become not to define our businesses in terms of how we deliver our products but for what purpose we make them.

CHAPTER 4

MYTH AND REALITY ON THE SUPERHIGHWAY

We now need to return to the simplification we introduced at the start of chapter 3. We pretended that the world of digital media was neatly divided into packaged media products – essentially bits embodied in atoms – and transmitted media products which are purely bits from the moment they are created to the moment they are delivered to their users. We have already seen in the past few pages that this kind of simple division is a highly artificial way of structuring digital media sectors and the reality is increasingly that packaged and transmitted media are beginning to merge to produce rich, hybrid publishing and distribution opportunities and a fundamentally new kind of experience for the users. However, we can as a matter of convenience and practical reality, maintain the fiction because while hybridisation is becoming increasingly important, most digital media developments still fall into one camp or the other. Our initial simplification, however, may soon get simpler. As we turn to consider transmitted media and the rise of the networks, we may well be studying the ultimate nemesis of CD-ROM media with hybrids merely a step on the road towards extinction. While we need to make the argument more fully, there is a strong case for believing that – except in niche applications such as digital video discs – the future of digital media is exclusively a wired one.

The notion of 'getting wired' is gaining common currency. One of the world's most successful new media magazines – admittedly one heavy with attitude and posturing – is actually called *Wired*. The metaphor suggests somehow gaining a physical cabled or wired connection to something – presumably a flow of information, entertainment and education. Leaving aside the issue of whether such physical connections are really needed, the underlying idea is important because it embodies an implicit reference to a term that has become one of the most widely used clichés of the media industry – 'the information superhighway'. The popular working understanding of the term is that it describes a vast, directed flux of digital information and communication carried amongst and to users in homes, schools, universities, institutions and offices throughout the world, consisting of the richest imaginable synthesis of text, sound, images – including video – and computer programs capable of delivering complete applications to remote computers and other appliances linked to the flux. In other words, the information superhighway is – partly, at least – a grand vision of a future in which the world is interactively connected to all the digital information and entertainment it wants – and then some. The implications of this 'wired' future are meant to include the emergence of major markets for hardware, software and content, all driving a new era of economic growth and prosperity in these sectors and – at a human level – creating an opportunity to fight ignorance, poor educational standards and ennui. In other words, a unique chance to enrich the world commercially and culturally. Through the power to use the superhighway as a conduit for communications as well as media distribution, it also becomes a means of breaking down barriers between peoples, getting nations to speak unto nations and ultimately, therefore, helping to build a single global community.

If you have managed to catch your breath, you will appreciate that this is a somewhat idealised vision of what digital networks may one day deliver. Of course, there is nothing wrong with an idealised vision of the future so long as we recognise it as an expression of hope and objective rather than a description of any kind of near-term reality. What lies behind this vision and, in practical terms, what does it demand in terms of infrastructure and technology development?

The source of the vision – perhaps surprisingly – is probably a politician. In 1993, Vice-President Al Gore continued work he had started as the senator for Tennessee by formulating the US Information Infrastructure Initiative. Among its many detailed provisions, the Initiative is particularly interesting because for the first time it raised the significance and priority of building coherent information infrastructures in the United States to the same level as maintaining and extending the US network of roads and highways, the physical arteries vital to the prosperity and functioning of the nation. It was entirely appropriate that Gore and his colleagues sought to link the Initiative to the US road-building programme in terms of national priority because the paradigm underpinning the Initiative was, of course, already widely referred to as the information superhighway.

THE BROADBAND VISION

As our previous description implies, the single technological concept underpinning the superhighway is the vision of plentiful, cheap bandwidth making it possible to link the nations of the world by means of a unified infrastructure of fast, interactive networks. This means networks that have three key ingredients: switching, bandwidth and pervasiveness. The last is less technological-driven than market-driven but has strong links to technology developments – after all, the only networks that can ever become pervasive are those that are cheap and friendly to use and fundamentally it is the efficiency of underlying technology and technological design which decides these things.

It is helpful to consider each of the three defining features of superhighway systems in turn to understand their significance and what their realisation actually means for the practical business of building the superhighway.

SWITCHING

We start with switching, the technology which is the fundamental source of the one-to-oneness (or many-to-manyness) of interactive networks. To understand this clearly, consider first a non-interactive network. The best example is a cable TV service. The physical infrastructure is designed, of course, to carry television programmes to a community of subscribers physically connected to the cabling of the network. A network of this kind has to have substantial bandwidth because it is carrying good quality, full screen video information. That is why cable TV networks are made from a combination of optical fibre and coaxial cable with the coaxial cable making the final drop to the individual houses connected to the system. But a cable television service is based on a broadcasting model. In other words, the same information is transmitted from the cable head end – the system which injects the television programming into the network – to every subscriber connected to the service. The only interactivity takes place when individual subscribers turn their televisions on or off and when subscribers select programmes by tuning their receiver into the appropriate frequency representing a particular channel's offerings. There is certainly no need for any return path by which subscribers can communicate with the head end or with any other subscribers. Cable television services, therefore, are purely non-interactive, point-to-multipoint systems.

Contrast this with a telephone network. Telephone services are fundamentally different from cable television because the reason they exist is to offer a means of two-way communication. Unlike broadcasting, where the communication is all one-way, telephones are for dialogue. In other words, telephone networks have to be designed to carry information from any user of the system to any other user of the system. There is no single head end, just millions of individual points of use. This means individual streams of such information – usually in the form of voice conversations – have to be routed through the network so they reach their intended recipients. And in order to ensure conversations do not grind to a halt, all this has to happen quickly. Telephone services, therefore, are point to point or multipoint to multipoint. They lie at the other end of the spectrum to conventional broadcasting systems.

The key technology which distinguishes these two kinds of networks is switching, a kind of traffic police force – usually consisting of sophisticated computer programs – which lives inside the network directing information hither and thither through its physical infrastructure so that it can reach its specified destination. In crude terms, cable television systems do not have switching because they do not need it. Telephone networks do have switching because they could not function without it.

This distinction is vitally important when we consider the creation of superhighways because, if we are ever going to build them, we are not going to snatch them out of thin air. We are going to evolve superhighways out of the existing infrastructure we have already spent billions putting into the ground. This means there are two main contenders for the heartland of the superhighway: cable television systems and telephone networks. This simplifies the actual reality because there are considerable opportunities to utilise the electromagnetic spectrum for non-material transmission links in the superhighway. But, for our immediate purposes, we can imagine that we are watching a two-horse race.

BANDWIDTH

This leads us to our second key element essential to a superhighway system – it has to have plenty of bandwidth. Indeed, for many, the idea of almost infinite capacity lies at the heart of the superhighway and distinguishes it from any other communications system that has ever been invented. In fact, the concept of infinite bandwidth – or at least the plentiful availability of cheap bandwidth – is a major defining feature of the digital age. Curiously, it is only partly to do with going digital. Dramatic increases in bandwidth – and the related reduction in its cost – are driven by two factors. One is compression – the possibility of making thin pipes fat and fat pipes fatter, not by changing their inherent character or composition but by squeezing digital information into less bandwidth. We have already discussed compression schemes in earlier chapters but it is worth reminding ourselves that this characteristic of digital information – its compressibility – is one of the most important single foundations of the digital media age. Compression therefore is one of the two factors that give us vastly more bandwidth than we have ever had from existing transmission systems. The other factor has nothing to do with the digital age in itself and is specific to the composition of the physical infrastructure and, accordingly, is peculiar to networks in the ground rather than those which use the electromagnetic spectrum in the air above our heads. The transforming development is the increasing availability of fibre optic cable as a component of physical networks.

It is hard to properly illustrate the leap in capacity which fibre optic technology offers. It is simply too huge to grasp. But we can try. Imagine that the entire population of the world decided simultaneously to have a conversation with itself – would that it would – and then double the amount of information this mega-conversation would generate. The amount of information you are left with could be transmitted – with room to spare – along a single filament of optical fibre no thicker than a human hair. Now consider that in real life a fibre optic cable is made from a huge bundle of such fibres and you will have some sense of the vastness of the capacity of a fully fibred network. To all intents, it is unlimited.

Life of course is never simple. It sounds as if the world's communications needs, at all levels from voice to interactive multimedia, could be solved by simply replacing all the copper currently in the ground with fibre. And naturally they could. However, fibre optic cable is costly – not merely in terms of the cable itself but because of the specialised expertise and technology needed to install, maintain and integrate it into existing communications infrastructures. As a result, most of the advanced communications networks in the world are today a hybrid mix of fibre and copper. The general principle guiding the deployment of fibre is a common-sense one. It is placed where bandwidth demands have traditionally been greatest. For example, in a telephone system, the major backbones that link large urban areas obviously carry a huge amount of traffic – all the calls typically bound for a whole city conurbation. Once the network reaches the destination city, however, it starts splitting its traffic into ever more local segments until it eventually gets down to the level of neighbourhoods, streets and individual houses or offices. Obviously, as the traffic splits down to local levels, its volume bound for any particular locality decreases and as this happens, the need for high bandwidth fibre declines. So the usual approach is to use fibre for the main trunks carrying traffic for large areas and then to introduce the much cheaper copper at more local levels. Note also that as the backbones split into a myriad of tributaries connecting localities, the amount of cabling needed soars. For typical networks of this kind, over 80 per cent of the physical infrastructure is invested at the street level, the final local drop to the end users.

This intensity of infrastructure at local levels – which simply follows from the logic of the way that such communications networks are organised – is crucial to the problem of turning existing networks into broadband ones. As we have seen, the networks are broadband already but only in parts. And – from the point of view of creating superhighways – they are the wrong parts. The backbones have hogged the fibre because, to use the network for its existing purposes, that is where the need is greatest. However, superhighways need high bandwidth end-to-end and specifically they need it at the most local level. When we are simply transmitting voice data back and forth locally, twisted pairs of copper wires with very limited capacity – as currently used in most telephone networks – are adequate for the ultimate connection between end users and the network. In a sense, the copper wire is the ultimate reducing valve through which information has to be squeezed – and to be squeezed in both directions, to and from end users.

Now the problem of turning telephone networks into broadband ones is clear. Because most of the physical infrastructure is concentrated into the local drop, the idea of simply running optical fibre through the whole network is a task of staggering proportions. The sheer quantity of fibre needed is huge and the barrier to proceeding is, therefore, cost. But cost, of course, is not a serious barrier if the fruits of the financial investment are sufficiently attractive. In other words, telephone networks – at least in the advanced countries of the world – would turn into fibre optic highways in the twinkling of an eye if the telephone companies could anticipate sufficiently rich financial rewards from making the necessary investments. We will return to this crucial idea shortly because – aside from the technological and engineering issues – it is market demand played off against investment costs that ultimately determines whether the vision of the superhighway ever gets turned into reality.

We have emphasised the problem that telephone networks face at local level. The bottleneck created by their copper wire connections to users is the main barrier which stands between them and the immediate realisation of a superhighway service. Now that the superhighway is an issue, therefore, it is not surprising that telephone companies are studying ways of prising open the bottleneck without having to invest in the huge amount of re-cabling that would otherwise be needed. The obvious answer, of course, is to use some kind of compression scheme to squeeze more information through the copper without having to replace it. Within the last few years, a scheme especially suited to making narrow copper wires seem fatter has emerged. Known as ADSL (asymmetric digital subscriber loop), this allows VHS quality video to be transmitted through the copper, to the user. Bandwidth for traffic originated by users is strictly limited – that is why the scheme is called 'asymmetric' – but the idea is that the only information that users will want to issue is brief requests or enquiries related to the content available to be delivered by the ADSL service. Although a limited solution, other more powerful versions of the original ADSL are under development and many US and European telephone companies are embracing it as an opportunity to cheat the limitation of their local loops without having to invest in rebuilding them. Currently, ADSL schemes are being widely tested. Critics argue that it is a compromise that costs too much and delivers too little. After all, they point out, it increases the bandwidth of the twisted pair of copper wires but falls short of creating true broadband performance. One or even a few channels of VHS quality video, or its equivalent in other services, is hardly the stuff of which superhighways are made. This may be true but the issue is not really one of technology at all. ADSL may have limitations but what really counts is whether it can deliver services that consumers will want at a price they will pay. The real determinant, therefore, is the market, not the particular choice of technology.

We should now turn to cable television networks again. All that we have said about fibre in communications networks has so far concentrated on telephone systems. And telephone systems are distinctive – as we have seen – because they are designed to handle low bandwidth voice traffic, connecting any user of the network with any other user. Cable television may have no return path – at least, within its television service – but it carries the kind of traffic that many expect to see on the superhighway. In other words, cable television networks are designed for delivering high quality video and are therefore inherently broadband systems. Bear in mind, however, that right now they are not digital. Unlike advanced telephone networks which went digital some years ago, most cable TV systems handle exclusively analogue information and will go digital only when cable operators judge that markets have emerged for use of expanded capacity – in particular, new bandwidth-hungry services like near-video-on-demand. But while cable networks are, by their nature, broadband, what they are not is two-way broadband systems. They have no return path.

In terms of infrastructure, they may well have plenty of fibre near the head end to get the programming content injected into the network quickly at high power but even as their system drops down to the local level, it still needs far more capacity than a telephone network. Even at the local drop, it is still utilising a fairly fat pipe, this time made out of copper coaxial cable rather than the thin metal wires of the telephone system. Even without a form of ADSL technology, the link with the user offers potentially plenty of bandwidth in both directions. Obviously, if the cable services went digital and applied a decent compression scheme they could increase this bandwidth still further and turn the coaxial drop into a mainstream multimedia connection. This leaves us with an interesting irony peculiar to the world's existing networks. The cable television services have the bandwidth but no switching while the telephone services have the switching but no bandwidth. Little surprise that in the early 1990s, the idea of strategic alliances between telephone and cable companies in the United States – where cable reaches over 60 per cent of the population – looked like natural marriages. Of course, the issues in reality went far deeper than infrastructure and – as the famous US West/TCI (Telecommunications Inc.) merger-that-never-was shows – there is much more to marriage than plugging networks together.

PERVASIVENESS

But telephone networks have one big advantage over cable which over-whelms even cable's massive (potential) bandwidth superiority. They are almost completely pervasive. Do you know anyone who does not have access to a telephone? In fact, this is a loaded question based on the fact that readers of this book can be assumed to be living in first world countries and enjoying a reasonably good standard of living in every sense – education, job, material possessions. The more global reality is that 60 per cent of the world's population has never made a phone call and more than 50 per cent could not do so because of a lack of phone lines. So, while we glibly agree that the telephone is the most widely available form of network technology in the world, we should – in a small corner of our minds – remember the privileged position from which we make such judgements. However, for the developed world at least, we can say with conviction that telephone networks do indeed have that vital ingredient that we suggested was vital to the superhighway – pervasiveness. Conversely, it is an ingredient that cable does not have – at least, not consistently. In the United States and some European countries, cable has a massive installed base. But even in such highly cabled territories, cable systems do not interconnect to form single, contiguous networks. We cannot subscribe to a single service – as we can with a phone – and gain access to the world – or even the whole of our own country. In other words, even if they may be extensive, cable television networks are usually organised on the basis of local franchises and subscribers can gain access only to the offerings of that franchise.

This appears to give telephone networks a clinching two out of three superhighway ingredients if it were not for the fact that, increasingly, cable systems are being made to interconnect with telephone networks. At the simplest level, this means no more than bringing with the coaxial cable connection into the home, a twisted pair copper line to carry voice telephone traffic. By doing this, cable companies – in the UK, in particular – have built a substantial business in telephony. In the UK, the national telephone company, British Telecom (BT), is obliged to provide cable operators with interconnect services which allow cable's local telephony loop – the copper wire delivered to their subscribers wrapped around the coaxial TV cable – to be switched into BT's national infrastructure. This has made it possible for UK cable to offer subscribers telephone services at lower rates than BT. As a result, cable in the UK – always in the shadow of BSkyB's satellite broadcast services – is now generating good revenues out of its telephone services and making cable sales purely on the basis of being able to offer lower telephony charges than any other provider. Although the provision of this kind of telephone service – an essentially narrowband link to the home running parallel to their broadband television service – can do no more than ordinary telephone networks to deliver interactive multimedia, we will see a little later in this chapter how the telephone facility can offer a powerful return path in order to build a degree of interactivity, even out of a broadcast system.

At a more powerful level, however, cable television systems are now being designed to act as a fat-pipe link into the faster thoroughfares of telephone networks. In other words, the hope is that the copper coaxial in the local drop of cable television can also act as a slip road into the parts of the telephone networks that are already fibred up to superhighway standards. The particular development which is causing interest at present is the prospect of turning existing narrowband networks – that is, computer networks using conventional telephone systems as their carriers – into multimedia networks by linking cable television not to television but to PCs. If this can be done, the powerful interactivity of the narrowband networks could be enhanced by the speed of coaxial pipes acting as fast lanes into the heart of the telephone system. Both to examine this in more detail and simultaneously to understand the difficult future facing the superhighway, we will look at the rise of what has been called 'PC Cable'. In fact, dealing with it now leapfrogs some of the detailed material we will be covering in chapter 5. So, vertical thinkers may find it easier to jump forward to read chapter 5 and then rewind to this point to get to grips with the prospects for a broadband/narrowband merger. Lateralists – or those who know something about online basics – can go straight ahead!

TAKING CABLE ONLINE

In the summer of 1995, news that Time Warner – second largest cable TV operator in the United States – was collaborating with Time Inc. on tests of a high speed consumer online service in the United States using part of Time Warner's cable TV system, seemed to suggest the first concrete step towards a bright new dawn for interactive broadband services – at least, those delivered to a PC screen. Subsequently, announcements by the largest cable operator, John Malone's Telecommunications Inc. (TCI), that it was deploying a similar cable-based service called @Home seemed to add confirmation. But the idea of using existing fat coaxial cables to deliver fast online services was not new. In 1993, for example, Steve Case, CEO of fledgling America Online – today a giant of the US online industry – claimed that the use of cable to link PCs to interactive services was the most important and exciting immediate prospect facing network operators and content providers. The vision was one of dramatic revolution where – with the right modems – online information delivery speeds could be raised from the maximum 28.8 kbs (thousand bits per second) of conventional telephone-based systems to the megabyte range (millions of bits per second – Mbps). Some forecasters predicted (and continue to predict) speeds of 30 Mbps and above – enough for interactive, real-time, broadcast quality video delivered to the PC screen.

For the first time, proponents of the PC screen as the natural meeting place for all interactive entertainment, education and information, could foresee the delights of high speed, online multimedia being delivered to millions of eager consumers without having to await the emergence of fully fibre optic superhighways. Seen through these particular rose-tinted spectacles, PC Cable – as it has quickly become known – looks like the answer to delivering every online investor's dream of the ideal interactive service.

Like most dreams, however, PC Cable is less promising when exposed to the light of the real world. Crucially, of course, PC Cable needs both cable and customers connected to cable to work. While in the United States, as we have noted, over 60 per cent of homes have such connections, the installed base in the rest of the world is patchy. In other words, PC Cable makes sense mainly in the States and a few European countries, and has much less potential – at least, for mainstream consumer markets – elsewhere in the world. In any event, creating a functioning PC Cable system is more complex than simply plugging PCs instead of TVs into cable networks. The problems begin where the whole idea of PC Cable starts – with the physical infrastructure itself.

As we have seen, networks have many components but, for simplicity, we can think of them as made up of backbones with branches that lead to local areas of use. The key regions of a network so far as managing high bandwidth interactive services are concerned are the backbones and branches which can carry very high volumes of traffic and the local loop, the drop off at local level to individual users which generally carries more modest volumes, depending on the numbers of users it services. This is the bottleneck which all information ultimately has to pass. It is also the physical region into which most wire or cable is concentrated. In other words, the local loop is the most intense area of infrastructure investment for networks of all kinds. Whether you are a telephone company or a cable TV operator, you may well upgrade your backbone with fibre optic cable to increase the capacity of your backbones as you get more traffic to handle. But you are unlikely to put fibre into the local loop because of the vast investment needed and because infinite bandwidth at local level is simply an overkill.

We have also seen (pp. 71–2) that there is a fundamental divide separating cable and telephone networks. The divide is based on a simple fact of life. Cable TV services have been devised to deliver broadcast applications. They work by beaming the same information to everyone – point to multipoint. Telephone companies, by contrast, are in a totally different business. Their networks are designed inherently to service point-to-point traffic. In other words, they are ideal for interactive services which need addressability in a network in order to send a particular bit of information to a particular location. What is obvious from this is that telephone networks have an ideal architecture for interactive services and cable TV networks do not. What is missing in the cable networks – as we have discussed – is the complex switching necessary to route particular bits of data to particular people who have indicated they want it.

However, if telephone companies have something cable needs – switching and addressability – cable has something that telephone companies want: plenty of bandwidth in the local loop. While the 'last mile' to the telephone user is invariably a low bandwidth connection made of a twisted pair of copper wires, cable TV networks use coaxial cable to the door. So the answer for cable if it wants to turn interactive looks simple: build in switching and create addressability. With that in place, it would be easy to start delivering interactive multimedia services over their fibre-coax networks. But again the reality is more complex. In order to put in switching, cable companies need to have network architectures that support the branching structures that lead to a local node and a local delivery loop. The most recent cable networks do have such architectures but they tend to exist in only modestly cabled territories – such as the UK. In long-established markets such as the United States, where millions of homes are connected to cable, the infrastructure is often old and the architecture wrong for today's interactive initiatives.

US cable majors such as Time Warner and Telecommunications Inc. have not been idle. Although their businesses are small in revenue terms compared with the telephone companies, they have been investing heavily in upgrading the architectures and infrastructure of their networks. In other words, more fibre is going into the ground and switchable architectures are being constructed. To make @Home work, for example, TCI is building a national high speed network backbone with the Internet at one end and regional data centres at the other. Located all over the United States – wherever TCI operates a cable network – the data centres will feed local hubs where dedicated @Home servers will be located. These computers will replicate and cache data to cut down the amount of traffic flowing through the backbone and will host frequently used data so that they are available as close as possible to the homes of @Home subscribers.

The message, therefore, is that cable has its problems but in the United States, at least, investment may be overcoming the technological limitations of the network.

But the problems for PC Cable run still deeper. The modems needed to handle megabits of information every second are difficult and traditionally expensive beasts. Majors such as Intel and General Instruments are co-operating on initiatives to produce a new generation of cheap, high speed modems but so far the only devices widely available cost – at the time of writing – well over $1,000 each. The price is coming down. General Instruments, for example, has announced a halfway house, a device priced at $300 called SURFboard which is a one-way cable modem. This provides multimedia into the PC via a 27 Mbps modem working in concert with an ordinary telephone modem which handles the much lighter upstream traffic initiated by the end user. Much progress is being made both techno-logically and in terms of industry co-operation. Most importantly, the US cable industry has recently agreed a new set of standards for cable modems which ensures that no longer will modems from different manufacturers work in different ways. Under the newly agreed standards, modem prices are likely to fall sharply with $500 considered attainable by the end of 1996 and $200 well before the end of the century.

However, raw cost is not the only issue. Cheap or expensive, cable modems are traditionally complex and difficult to install. Average con-sumers are unlikely to be happy to fiddle for hours with incomprehensible system adjustments in order to make their modem work with the PC Cable service. This means that PC Cable operators may have to train and deploy a specialised workforce of technicians to visit subscribers and set up their systems. Together with the inevitable return visits for debugging and maintenance, this new workforce could represent a huge additional investment for operators.

Even if we overcome all these barriers, we are left with another couple of bear traps. Even if the system works well, it will necessarily pay the price of conveying sensitive digital data over coaxial cable. While it has plenty of bandwidth, coax is not a clean pipe. Even in the latest cables, noise is often introduced during transmission. While this is not important if all you are sending is analogue (or even digital) television signals, it is crucially important for online services. The occasional bit dropping out of an online signal could totally deform the information delivered or – more dangerously – introduce subtle but fundamental errors. Imagine checking your bank balance and finding an extra zero on the bottom line! Expensive error correction will be vital to make sure the online dream does not become a nightmare of liability suits. In addition, the speed that cable can actually deliver may not be as great as anticipated. In the final path from the local data head end to the home, information is planned to take up bandwidth equivalent to a single TV channel. But every house on the local drop – which can vary from a few hundred to a few thousand homes – will have to share this bandwidth. This means that the speed experienced by each individual user will depend on how many other users are online at the same time. If a large number of homes choose to use the system at one time, the whole service could grind to a halt. Even moderate losses of speed or constant variations could play havoc with an entertainment service designed for users who are generally not hardened veterans of PC services with a natural tolerance of glitches. The cable operators have an easy answer. If the system is so successful that it starts slowing down in average use, they will consider dropping one of their other TV channels to make more bandwidth available. But this would mean losing one source of revenue – the pay-TV channel they sacrifice – to gain another. In other words, the final decision will be made by deciding whether the PC cable service is profitable enough to be worth the sacrifice. Of course, when cable TV goes fully digital and can begin compressing the programming it carries, it will have plenty of bandwidth to spare. In other words, the issue may be relatively short-term, depending on when the move to digital broadcasting is taken.

All these barriers are essentially technological. There are ways to overcome them even if there is a price – and a high one – to be paid. The most fundamental barrier, however, has little to do with the technology in itself. It has to do with the customer. It is just possible that the people who subscribe to cable TV and who may also want to buy online services are less excited about the incorporation of full screen, good quality video than the proponents of PC Cable think. For example, VHS quality video in a window on the screen will soon be available and 'good enough' to enrich many online applications. Real-time sound – as we will see when we examine narrowband online services in more detail – is already a possibility through new software such as RealAudio. Well ahead of the commercial rise of PC Cable, speed and capacity is increasing by leaps and bounds on the narrowband networks. True, the 'speed of light' for networks still remains the bottleneck into the home or office of the end user. The local loop is an issue. But we are already seeing new software-based compression technologies emerging that will make it possible to squeeze ever more data through the bottleneck. And if compression is not good enough on its own to do everything that customers want, then there are ways of cheating bandwidth restrictions altogether by sending only low resolution instructions over the network and getting the user's computer to do the processing necessary to create the desired broadband experience. A good example of this trend is the new tools derived from Virtual Reality Modelling Language which can turn an online connection into a kind of construction set which uses its host computer to build at a local level a three-dimensional experience from basic, narrowband instructions delivered over the network. One way or the other, 'good enough' multimedia may soon be available without the need to fight through the raft of technological and commercial obstacles which can prevent PC Cable working.

So the last barrier for PC Cable to surmount is probably the toughest. We summed it up above by using the phrase 'good enough' multimedia. Even if PC Cable becomes a technical and commercial reality and even if it delivers network speeds to the user in the order of millions of bits per second, there remains the fundamental question of what to do with such formidable bandwidth and what services customers will want to buy. What can such PC-based broadband services deliver that enhanced narrowband services cannot do now – or in the near future – well enough to satisfy customers? Currently, cable operators believe that users will want to view programming more than interact with it. But can we really imagine a generation of US cable subscribers asking 'What's on the PC tonight, honey?' The reality facing broadband proponents pushing PC Cable forward is that customers may find little to attract them which they cannot get on conventional online services, unless they want to watch movies on their PC screens. Of course, they might want to do just this but even if they do, will they want to do it often enough and at a high enough price for movies and TV programming on demand to be an economic driver for the service?

Where does this leave PC Cable? Certainly an exciting possibility for consumer markets but with many barriers yet to surmount and an ultimate question mark about its competitive edge over other, fast-improving delivery systems. In other niche sectors which demand the high quality imaging of video which only true broadband systems can supply, PC Cable obviously has much to offer. If the numbers work for the cable operators and investment can be justified, PC Cable could yet find successful applications in health care, medicine, public access kiosks with live video-conferencing and, of course, video-conferencing more generally. The drawback for cable operators, of course, is that their expensive networks currently pass homes more frequently than they do corporate offices and professional institutions. In other words, it is conceived largely as a consumer technology.

How does all of this affect conventional narrowband services, online networks based on existing telephone networks? The answer, of course, is clear and encouraging for players in this sector. Narrowband – as we will see when we look at the market in more detail in chapter 5 – is established and is both deepening and widening its installed base. It relies on a truly pervasive international network system – the telephone line. It is also providing increasingly faster access through its existing infrastructure. We have already discussed the use of compression technology such as ADSL to improve the bottleneck at the local loop but even without compression, the use of protocols such as ISDN (Integrated Services Digital Network) can offer dramatic improvements in local speed. Currently, ISDN is too expensive to be used for anything other than business applications but prices are falling and in high volume markets such as the United States, there is a real possibility that ISDN connections at a price that homes can afford will be a commonplace reality by the end of 1997. In Europe, the process will be much slower but even in these markets ISDN prices are falling. Indeed, many commentators now believe that battlelines are being drawn between PC Cable and ISDN with both offering the potential for fast access to online services. The proponents of cable modems believe that cable will offer greater speed at lower prices. Champions of ISDN simply do not believe that cable can deliver the goods it promises and that ISDN is a more reliable technology for, at least, the medium-term future. But with or without enhancements such as ISDN, narrowband networks are anyway increasingly capable of delivering multimedia experiences to their users. This is the crucial fact that represents the greatest threat to fledgling developments in the cable industry. If you look at the interplay between PC Cable initiatives and narrowband networks as a contest, therefore, there simply isn't one.

MAKING BROADCASTING INTERACTIVE

We have spent a good deal of time discussing superhighway issues in terms of physical infrastructure – bandwidth buried in the ground in the form of various kinds of cables. But there is, of course, bandwidth in the sky. Sections of the electromagnetic spectrum have been used since the turn of the century for communications. Since the birth of radio and television, other parts of the spectrum have been packed with broadcast entertainment, information and education. Until recently, such broadcasting has been exclusively analogue but, now, in the final years of the twentieth century, we are watching the inevitable shift taking place. Broadcasting is going digital.

We have already noted some of the implications of this shift. We have, for example, shown how compression can expand the capacity of satellite television broadcasting, multiplying the number of channels which can be distributed from satellite transponders and providing the basis for the first near-video-on-demand (NVOD) services. When we introduced the idea of NVOD in chapter 2, we did so to emphasise the power of digital-compression to reshape service offerings and to commercialise a new way of delivering traditional media experiences – in this case, television programmes. However, we can also begin to see in the concept of broadcast near on-demand services the prospect of a fully interactive publishing model, even though the underlying technology is not based on one-to-one communications. After all, so long as a service which is technically 'near on-demand' delivers something which its users experience as 'on-demand', it is mere semantics to argue whether or not it is 'truly' one-to-one interactive or not.

Consider the workings of a NVOD service. Such a service could be delivered by any broadcasting system. The only fundamental requirement is plenty of bandwidth because NVOD works by wasting masses of capacity, broadcasting over and again the same programming but time-shifted slightly to give alternative, shoulder-to-shoulder start times. The user switching on at any moment of the day would find the desired programme about to start on at least one of the broadcast channels being used by the NVOD system. On the face of it, NVOD is purely a broadcast system with no return path. But, of course, as a commercial enterprise it has to have some means for subscribers to say which videos they want to view simply to be able to charge them for the privilege of using the service.

To understand how this is done – and to appreciate why this is the key to making broadcasting interactive – it is important to know how a pay-

TV service works, whether it is based on satellite, cable or terrestrial services. The fundamental idea underpinning any paid-for television service is simple. Those who have paid to receive the service must be permitted to receive it while those who have not paid must be prevented from receiving it. In conventional 'free TV', of course, no such issue arises. All you need is a television aerial (or satellite dish) and a television receiver. Tune the receiver to the right frequency and you can enjoy the television being broadcast freely to anyone who wants it. The business model for such services is based on generating revenue either from advertisers or – in some countries – from licence fees levied on the viewing population. Pay-TV sometimes utilises advertising but also derives substantial income from subscribers who either buy unlimited access to one or more channels or buy on some form of pay-per-view basis. Whichever way it works, pay-TV requires some kind of gatekeeper to allow access only to those who have paid for the privilege. The most common form of gatekeeper is a conditional access system, half of which is built into a set-top box which sits between the incoming television signal and the user's television receiver. The other half of the system lies in the hands of the broadcaster and is a proprietary form of scrambling which jumbles the television picture and makes it impossible to view. The scrambling is controlled by a mathematical algorithm which acts much like a key locking access to the unscrambled pictures. The algorithm is a form of encryption and ownership of it defines the proprietary control that the broadcaster can exert over the pay-TV service. If it falls into the wrong hands or can be replicated in some way, people who have not paid for services could figure out how to decrypt the TV signals and unlock them for normal viewing. Not surprisingly, there is a lively trade in pirate versions of decryption systems designed to break into pay-TV broadcasts. The decryption in legitimate set-top boxes relies on a smart card supplied by the pay-TV operator which fits into the set-top box and allows the incoming signal to be decrypted and unscrambled. Operators change their decryption regularly and supply sub-scribers with updated cards. Pirates try to keep up with the changes and sell cut-price cards that do the same thing as the legitimate ones.

We used the word gatekeeping above advisedly because the card in the set-top box represents a strategically very powerful form of gate. Consider a dominant satellite operator such as BSkyB in the UK. It has between 3 million and 4 million subscribers. Each has a BSkyB set-top box equipped with a single slot designed to take BSkyB's proprietary decryption card. It is highly unlikely that any other satellite operator is going to be able to sell any other set-top boxes to such UK viewers and BSkyB, therefore, has a captive audience tied to its boxes and cards. This means, effectively, that any programme producer or channel operator wishing to sell pay-TV services to the UK market has first to do business with BSkyB. If they do not, they have no way of getting through the proprietary gate which

BSkyB has introduced into the UK consumer market. So, whatever services we might wish to formulate for satellite broadcasting – whether conventional or near on-demand – we will have to formulate as part of a deal with BSkyB.

The interesting feature of this situation is that it applies widely to any service which is based on placing a proprietary 'box' or other digital access technology into the hands of service users. The proprietary character of the access technology defines the 'gate' and the installed base of the gate, the penetration that it achieves in its target market, determines the commercial influence that it can wield to shut out competitors. Underlying this is a crucial power play among top media and software companies to establish dominant positions. Whether they do this by ensuring that everyone uses their computer interface or by putting their proprietary set-top box in lots of homes, the central ploy is to create and own a gate that arbitrates access to a world of content or applications which people want to pay for. Of course, gatekeeping of this kind is a balancing act aimed at achieving commercial control without upsetting regulators by stretching anti-competition laws too far.

Leaving aside this more general context, however, we also need to understand another important feature of the set-top boxes which perform the role of gatekeeping technology for pay-TV services. Not only are they gatekeepers to allow access to services to those who have paid, but also they are individually addressable. In other words, they each contain an individual digital identifier which makes it possible for a broadcaster to communicate uniquely with a single chosen box. This is a crucial idea because it means that while the same communication must, of course, go to every set-top box owner, only a selected box will respond to the special message addressed to it. This addressability is already routinely used to update software in set-top boxes to give subscribers new services they have requested or to switch off those who have not paid their bills.

The fact that set-top boxes are individually addressable now allows us to extend the idea of NVOD into a fully interactive information service based entirely on a broadcast model. NVOD works by subscribers selecting a video to watch by making a telephone call. The telephone line, therefore, is the return path. However, the call can easily be made automatically and transparently from the set-top box – so long as it is connected to a phone line. In other words, the user could simply use a remote control handset to select an on-screen option. The selection is then transferred to the set-top box which automatically calls the NVOD computer and lodges the request. The experience of the user is of making a screen selection and receiving the service a few minutes later. A personalised message to the user could precede the showing of the chosen programme just to enhance the sense of one-to-oneness. The fact that millions of other people are being sent the same message is irrelevant because none of them can view it.

Now consider how this model could be extended to provide more wide-ranging services than NVOD. Imagine the digitally broadcast signals from a satellite as a bitstream containing not only television signals but also multimedia databases. These databases would be transmitted in a compressed form so that they are distributed quickly and their transmission would continue like an endless loop, the same data being broadcast over and again without a break except for updating the database when necessary. A subscriber to the database service could make individual searches or selections by clicking on words or on-screen options. Their response would be instantly signalled to the service provider by the telephone link and their set-top box will subsequently be able to pick out of the bitstream only the information it is due, because that information will carry the unique code which addresses that one box and no others. In this way, a broadcasting system can be turned into a fully interactive experience without the need for the huge costs of building new physical infrastructures or updating old ones. The only major development required is for broadcasting to go digital so that bandwidth becomes cheaply available to accommodate such new services.

To an extent, we do not even need to wait until services go digital. It is already possible to transmit streams of digital data in the 'gap' between television frames transmitted in the conventional way. This gap – effectively an area of spare bandwidth – is known as the vertical blanking interval and is already widely utilised in non-interactive teletext services, particularly in Europe. The key to turning teletext interactive is to add a return path. The individual addressability of TV receivers is supplied not by a conditional access system in a set-top box, but by the teletext software inside the TV receiver itself. In the UK, BSkyB has already planned to extend the teletext model, even before its broadcasting goes digital, and has added a telephone return path to turn teletext into an interactive proposition. The same approach has been used in Scandinavia and Germany to create interactive games and classified advertising services.

This analysis of techniques of making broadcasting interactive emphasises an important fact about the superhighway. It is, above all, far from ever being a single, integrated technological entity. It can – and will – be built from a wide variety of ingredients ranging from enhanced telephone networks to ingenious reworkings of broadcasting systems. And it will be built piecemeal as a process of evolving and enhancing existing infrastructures rather than leaping fully formed into the world. Ultimately, of course, the deciding force determining what kind of superhighway is built, and whether broadband services ever become truly pervasive, has less to do with technology than with the needs and wishes of paying customers.

PAYING FOR THE SUPERHIGHWAY

The only people who will ever fund the superhighway are customers. So its future is dependent not merely on the power of technology but on its ability to deliver experiences which customers of all kinds will want to pay for. And they will need to be prepared to pay a price high enough to justify not only the commercial investments needed to build the super-highway but also the cost of maintaining it and tempting content companies to create the products and services which will bring it to life. When the idea of the superhighway was first explored, the vision overwhelmed all sense of reality. There was a 'build it and they will come' philosophy, which can be admirable when you are risking a few dollars of investment but madness when billions are at stake.

When the concept of the superhighway was still fresh, corporate excitement in the United States largely overwhelmed commercial prudence and cable companies and telephone companies rapidly began deploying trials of broadband initiatives. Most spectacular of these was Time Warner's full service network in Florida. Time Warner's initiative embodies so much investment that some commentators believe that its bid to create the net-work is tantamount to betting the company on the belief that the super-highway can be turned into a near-term commercialisable reality. By any standards, it is a big gamble. What makes it now look an even bigger one is the results of most of the other trials. It would be wearisome to detail them all but the bottomline is consistent. Leaving aside engineering and technical issues – which were generally found to be far more demanding than had been anticipated – the really worrying news was that consumers on the whole seem unwilling to pay economic prices for the kinds of services being offered. The centrepiece of the trial services was usually some form of video-on-demand (VOD). Unlike the NVOD systems that we have already examined, true VOD is a genuinely one-to-one interaction with a movie or TV programme being requested by an individual user and being instantly transmitted. Before the trials began bringing proponents of VOD in touch with reality, it had been widely seen as the 'killer appli-cation' of the superhighway – at least, in consumer markets. The reality was very different. While buy rates were certainly higher than conventional pay-per-view services, they were not nearly high enough. Perhaps even more telling was evidence that consumers were also unwilling to pay high premiums per view for the convenience of being able to select their viewing on-demand. Indeed, the implication of the trials so far is that near on-demand services – so long as the wait time is short between transmissions of programmes – are attractive enough and can be priced attractively enough to make them a sound commercial proposition, at least when broadcasting goes more widely digital. The reason, of course, illustrates the sandy foundations on which the superhighway vision is built. The bottomline is not technological excellence – although it is important. Neither is it political and commercial will – which is vital. Nor the willingness of content owners such as Hollywood studios to risk their huge rental and sell-through video revenues (more than twice their box office receipts per annum) on a new, competitive force in the market – although this is a crucial and little explored issue among service developers. The bottomline is the attitude of paying customers and their unwillingness to pay too much for too little. The reason near on-demand looks a distinct commercial possibility is because its infrastructure demands are much cheaper to satisfy and services can therefore be offered at prices customers may be willing to pay for the utility they receive. Broadband on-demand services, by contrast, are vastly more expensive to implement – at least, as originally conceived by superhighway proponents – and customers simply do not find the higher pricing of such services worth the added convenience that on-demand provides.

We have emphasised VOD because this is the kind of service which has been the centrepiece of most trials. But there are other services that broadband can offer – such as home shopping, banking services and multiplayer gaming. All these would be strong contenders for the future of superhighway development if it were not that classic narrowband counterparts are increasingly able to deliver many of the functionalities that broadband can offer. And the additional features unique to broadband – such as its unchallenged ability to handle full screen video in real-time – do not appear to be strong enough added values in themselves to justify broadband's immense additional cost.

While this case seems demonstrably true for the consumer market, it may not be so for niche business and professional applications. The underlying factors, however, are the same whatever sector we consider. If broadband – and only true broadband – can deliver a product or service which a market sector will buy at a sufficiently high price to make a limited broadband deployment profitable, then a market opportunity exists and will doubtless be exploited. This means we will certainly see segments of the superhighway emerging for applications local to the needs of particular sectors. Obvious near-term possibilities exist, for example, in the areas of public access multimedia kiosks for retailing, information and remote financial services, medicine and health care – where high quality, fast imaging can be vital – and in professional media applications requiring the rapid interactive transfer of high resolution pictures and video.

The future of the original superhighway vision, therefore, is being radically modified by the economic realities of the consumer market-place. Customers, as ever, are calling the tune. The concept of the commercial and governmental communities simply picking up their tools one day and building the superhighway is now widely seen as a naïve and idealist dream, out of touch with the wishes of the customers who are ultimately the commercial lifeblood of all such developments. The truth is that the superhighway is being built – despite all the evidence of the broadband trials. But it is being built by evolution rather than revolution. What we are seeing in the systematic enhancement of narrowband network services, the efforts to link cable television to telecommunications and the prospects of turning broadcasting into an interactive medium, is commercial and technological development trying to keep pace with the wishes of the customer, upgrading offerings only in ways in which the price of the added value will remain attractive to the customer. In other words, we are finding ways of edging our way towards the ultimate superhighway – the global, switched, broadband future – by leveraging the proven technologies of today at a price that both the commercial community and their customers are willing to pay. This incremental process also means that we are all getting the breathing space to learn an important lesson without having to bet the ranch like Time Warner is doing in Florida. We are finding out what kind of interactive services people really want and how, where and when they want to use them. This is not a trivial issue. Indeed, it is the bedrock of the interactive media market-place.

INTERACTIVE TELEVISION

It may seem surprising that throughout this chapter we have not once used the term 'interactive television'. It has been avoided – though implicitly discussed – because it is a confusing and unnecessary combination of words. Television is not interactive. Television is an established linear medium. In the digital age we can add value to the way that we deliver the traditional media experience – through NVOD, VOD and DVD, for example – but it remains (thankfully) the same satisfying linear experience it has always been. Interactive television (ITV), in so far as it means anything, suggests not so much a revision of the television programming experience but a reshaping of what people can do via their television receiver. In other words, ITV is the delivery of a range of interactive services, alongside traditional linear ones, to the television screen rather than the PC, something we have been examining for much of this chapter. This means that ITV is today really a kind of shorthand for a debate about whether PC and TV screens are converging. It is a complex argument. One response to it among companies that should know better is to produce PCs that are also televisions or televisions that are also PCs. This of course misses the point. The TV screen – designed as it is for middle-distance viewing – is largely unsuited for high resolution interactive services. More important – because technological design can always be varied – is the social and personal environment in which television is experienced. There is a simple and universal truth at work in the living rooms of the world. In the bosom of their home, the vast majority of people, stretched out in front of their television screens, are simply seeking fun and relaxation. Interactivity – beyond selecting channels or using the on-off switch – is simply too much like hard work.

While ingrained cultural behaviour can change – as anything can – over a long period of time, it looks, therefore, as if we can envisage a medium-term future in which television screens are used largely for traditional linear media experiences – perhaps with the added values of some near on-demand services – while PC screens remain the natural venue for interactive services, narrow-, mid- and ultimately broadband.

CHAPTER 5

ONLINE NETWORKS

In this chapter we will examine the rise of traditional online networks and the remarkable transition they are making in terms of the kinds of experiences that they can now deliver to their users. We will look at the changing strategies of online publishers and the emergence of important new business models for generating revenue and margin from online activities. A single, unifying thread is that we will take online to mean the use (predominantly) of traditional telecommunications systems for delivering interactive services. In other words, we are examining narrowband networks linking customers using computers.

HOW ONLINE PUBLISHING WORKS

The narrowband online industry is not new. In fact, it is the oldest and richest sector of the electronic media industry. Although our attention in recent years has been grabbed by the headlines about the rapid growth of CD-ROM markets, revenues generated by all forms of packaged media still remain – despite recent growth – small compared to online. By the end of 1995, the world market was probably worth $14 billion compared to a total for CD-ROM titles of about $3.5 billion. The difference is that online has taken 30 years to reach its current level while CD-ROM was invented only 10 years ago (1985).

In fact, the history of the online industry is of a slow and faltering business model which, for some years, looked as if it was running into a commercial dead end. We will not go into the details of that history now but we can establish some basic understanding of how online works today by examining some of the key factors determining the past developments in this sector. Most important of these is how online has attempted to leverage the unique attributes of digital information delivered over a one-to-one network and what we can learn from this about current and future business models in this sector. Before we look at these unique features, it will be useful to clarify what an online network is and how the traditional business model for online publishing works.

There are three important elements to a commercial online system. At its heart is the information to be commercialised. This is hosted as a structured database on a host computer. The host is the basic repository which is drawn upon to provide customers with the information they need. Attached to the host (or sometimes a part of the same computer) is the server. This provides the computing power needed both to regulate the flow of incoming enquiries and to inject responses into the network. The host–server system is linked by an ISDN or faster line into the telephone network which acts as the link with customers. In the jargon of the industry, the computers that customers use to connect themselves to the online service are termed clients. In practice they are usually conventional desktop PCs equipped with a modem to allow an exchange of digital data over the telephone network. Each client is given an identification code and some access software by the online publisher which allow it to dial up the service and make contact with the server and host computers. The client can, in principle, be anywhere in the world where there is access to a telephone line. In practice, operators of online services often establish a distributed network of subsidiary servers in key cities which feed the central server and host. The advantage of doing this is that it means clients need dial up only their most local server and this cuts telephone bills substantially. For example, a client in London using a particular online service may be accessing a host physically located in the United States. If the client has to make direct contact with the host, the client has to pay the cost of the telephone connection. This would make it unlikely that such a US host would have many UK clients. But if the online publisher has built points of presence in Europe and, in particular, in London, the client needs to make only a local call to get into the online system. The telecommunications charges between London and the United States still have to be paid, of course, but in this case they are absorbed by the online publisher and reflected in the charges to the client. This shifting around of telecommunications charges is important because online service operators can negotiate special bulk rates for long-distance phone traffic because they bring to the telephone companies a large number of individual users. This means they can get access to long-distance telephony at a fraction of the cost to individual users and make the process of intercontinental online communication relatively painless.

The traditional business model for an online publishing operation of this kind is usually based on a single strand of revenue generation. Customers subscribe to a service, usually for an annual payment, and are then charged for access to the service on a pay-as-you-go basis. Specifically, charges are most commonly calculated on the length of time that a user is actually online to the service. This process of connect-time charging is increasingly giving way to other forms of access deals but still remains the backbone of the industry.

THE UNIQUENESS OF ONLINE NETWORKS

Now we should return to the key attributes of online information which form the basis of the commercial offerings of these services. There are five really important ones:

- Infinite storage
- Searchability
- Real-time updating
- Global access
- Communications

INFINITE STORAGE

The database hosted by an online system can be huge. It is constrained only by the memory of the host computer and since such memory can always be extended by simply bolting on some more hard disk, the database can effectively be any size you want. Massive databases can offer a comprehensiveness in a given subject area that no other medium can match and this can be a persuasive feature in such areas as law, medicine or engineering, for example, where access to all available information can sometimes be the difference between success and professional disaster. However, size can bring its own problems. Simply because there are no real constraints on the size of the database or databases hosted, the publisher, in pursuit of comprehensiveness, may allow the product to become too large. Indeed, because comprehensiveness can become such a strong issue, online publishers in the past have gone to extremes, including much material that is never likely to be accessed. This leads to unnecessarily large databases, requiring users to make ever more lengthy and elaborate searches in order to find what they want. It has also meant that many databases that should never be issued commercially have found their way into the online industry. As a result, for most of its 30 years, online has been a slow-growing business characterised by terrabytes of unwanted and unused data clogging up computer memories all over the world. In other words, the lack of constraint on size sometimes led to a lack of editorial discipline in designing the products and a lot of bad publishing.

SEARCHABILITY

Online information is, of course, searchable. Comprehensiveness is hardly a benefit if users cannot get exactly what they want out of the data mountain, quickly and accurately. The key to this is the search and retrieval software provided to users. This software is effectively the electronic pair of hands which sift the data and locate or correlate information to give users the answers they need. The way the software works, the kinds of searches it can perform and the interface through which the user communicates with it, largely define the power of the online product.

REAL-TIME UPDATING

Online data can be updated on a moment-by-moment basis. This means that online publishing can provide access to fast-changing, time-critical information. In the late 1980s, it was this key feature that transformed the online industry. Up to then, the kinds of databases held online were largely historic in character. In other words, the currency of the information did not change much over time. Then a major transformation reshaped equity, commodity and currency markets as financial centres all over the world became computerised. Known jocularly as 'the big bang' it had very serious implications for international traders handling transactions often valued in billions. Access to the most up-to-date financial information – the raw data of fluctuating exchange rates, commodity values, stock prices – was vital to their competitiveness. In order to make the right judgements at the right times, traders had to pay whatever it might cost to get moment-to-moment feeds of information. Suddenly, online data came into their own purely because of their instant updatability; real-time financial information services exploded as a new and burgeoning sector of the otherwise moribund and slow-growing online industry. Such services carried very high price tags but the value they delivered was commensurately high. After all, a transaction worth many millions could depend on the intelligence delivered by such a service. Its price, therefore, was almost irrelevant.

By the end of the 1980s, nearly 70 per cent of all online revenues were generated by such services. Today, the proportion has settled at around 60 per cent. Although the real-time financial information services are a vitally important sector, they represent a large but specialist niche. However, they illustrate how a single unique feature of online data can be richly commercialised if the economic need exists in the market-place. They also suggest an important message for the future of online publishing. Online is good at delivering access to fast-changing information. This has value in itself in many sectors beyond international finance. Although we will touch on this in more detail later, it is worth noting now that even at a consumer level there is much time-critical information that users value – sports, weather, travel information, for example – and in designing services for these markets, even though they are radically different from such niches as finance and more general business applications, online's incomparable ability to deliver volatile information should always come high on the list of features to exploit. It is also worth remembering that access to volatile information not only delivers operational value to those who need the up-to-date-ness but also – where it is important as a sales proposition –

conveys a dynamic experience to its users. This can be a key feature in exciting and retaining interest among users, particularly in consumer markets.

GLOBAL ACCESS

Online services recognise no territorial boundaries. Just as we can make telephone calls all over the world thanks to the interconnection of national telephone networks, so we can access online systems from anywhere we can get a phone line. Apart from the unprecedented market reach this gives online services, it also has striking implications for the rights to exploit content. Traditionally such rights are defined by such criteria as the particular form of exploitation intended, the length of time the right to exploit subsists and in which territories – defined by geography or language or both – the exploitations may take place. Online services – particularly those hosted in environments such as the Internet where it is hard (though not impossible) to lock out particular territorial users – place real strain on conventional rights agreements and are pushing such deals towards routinely incorporating a global approach to the licences they embody. There are, of course, other more complex legal issues such as jurisdiction – particularly where a liability issue would be interpreted differently under different jurisdictions. The obvious issue would be to decide whether illegality took place where the server is located, where the user was when infringing material was accessed or whether the passage of material across the network constituted some kind of moving, international infringement. But, aside from these issues, most online publishers are attracted by the ease with which they can reach international markets. Reach is not the same thing as results, of course, and while networks can span the globe, it is still a major challenge for nationally based services to market their online products effectively on the international stage. The issue, however, is vastly different from having to ship material products like books or CD-ROMs where a traditional distribution value chain has to be commercialised. In the world of online networks the product is in the form of bits not atoms, and distribution in the traditional sense is no longer as important an issue as signalling to the market that you exist, have something to offer and are available from any nearby phone.

COMMUNICATIONS

Finally, online systems can provide communication as readily as they can provide content. This should not be surprising since they utilise networks dedicated to offering one-to-one conversations. But traditionally, this attribute has been the least exploited. The reason is obvious when we look back on the origins and early development of online publishing. The original business objective of such systems was to make access to information available to users on a commercial basis. On the whole, therefore, they were viewed exclusively as publishing operations with little interest in leveraging networks other than as distribution channels – albeit interactive ones – for content. The online systems were therefore configured in the form of a central server with clients accessing the hosted information bolted onto or a part of the server. Electronic mail, of course, was already becoming an accepted part of corporate local area networks – as distinct from wide area commercial publishing networks. But even electronic mail was not the point. Such mail was no more than a messaging service, valuable to be sure, but a million miles away from stranding the kinds of communications experiences into online activity that one day will create true virtual communities bound together not by operational synergies – as in corporate systems – or by geographical locality – as in most real-world communities – but by common interest, aspiration or belief. Increasingly, this notion of virtual community created by the communications power of networks is becoming the key to building a thriving new wired world.

THE EVOLUTION OF THE ONLINE INDUSTRY

With so much happening today, we should not dwell too much on history. But history is neither bunk nor boring. Above all, it provides invaluable context. A picture of how online publishing has evolved in recent years tells us much about the way it works today and suggests how it might develop in the future.

We have already touched on some of the past trends so we can afford to be brief and provide just the headlines. First, however, we need to emphasise a key distinction between the majority of commercial online networks in the past and a particular and distinctive network environment – the Internet – that has become of overwhelming importance in the 1990s. The distinction is that, before the emergence of the network as a global publishing and communications phenomenon, online was a world of proprietary networks. In other words, services were kept technically distinct – so that only those paying for access could use them – and were specifically designed for their customers. By contrast, the Internet was created to meet a particular non-commercial need amongst highly computer-literate users – mainly academics and researchers with an urgent desire to exchange information, research threads and ideas with colleagues in other institutions anywhere in the world. No single commercial organisation decided to create the Internet and no such organisation, therefore, can claim to own it. The Internet's software protocols – the technical infrastructure which makes it work and is largely responsible for what it can do – are available to anyone who is interested in them. That is why there is such a massive industry today amongst individual organisations selling various flavours of Internet access software, usually packaged with Internet access. Because the Internet was designed not by ordinary folk but by people who understood computers, it is an unfriendly and complex environment, only now beginning to be tamed for a wider constituency to use. Neither is it surprising that it is proving so difficult to build structures on the Internet to allow the secure trading of services and products. The Internet was never conceived or designed for the purpose. Proprietary networks on the other hand – if they are wisely implemented – can be made simple and attractive to use and optimised from the outset for commercial exploitations.

It is ironic, however, that the early online services were actually anything but easy to use. Indeed, in the 1970s and for much of the 1980s, the available networks were hard to access, difficult to navigate and expensive. Not a cocktail designed to promote rapid growth and, sure enough, growth was slow and unsteady. The reason why the original proprietaries were so unsatisfactory by today's standards was not a reflection of commercial incompetence but a natural result of the primitive state of computing and telecommunications. Surveys in the early 1980s, for example, demonstrated that one of the reasons why customers resisted using online services was because of the difficulty of logging on. And logging on was difficult simply because telephone connections often did not work, or worked and then broke down in the middle of the online session. In Europe, during this period, as many as one-third of all online transactions were aborted because users could not make the telephone call needed to secure an online connection.

Even if users managed to make a stable connection, their problems were only just beginning. The databases offered were typically very large and the search and retrieval engines were accordingly extremely powerful. But power brings its downside – particularly in the Stone Age of the early 1980s. Because the search systems had to perform complex tasks they were difficult to use. The command languages needed to make them search quickly and accurately were unfriendly and difficult to learn. The problem was compounded by the cost of using the services. Connect-time was priced very highly and forced users to get in and out of the databases as fast as possible in order to minimise charges. This placed added pressure on being able to drive the search software efficiently. The usual solution, still common today, was to use trained intermediaries skilled in using a range of search engines, to carry out the searches for the actual end users of the information. In other words, those needing the answers had to convey their questions to the intermediaries who would plan and devise a suitable search strategy to sift the required information from the online database. Once they were sure of the strategy they would log on and plunge into the database, grab the results of their search and log off. Needless to say, this was the framework for a low volume, high priced publishing business aimed at academic, corporate and professional users with a very strong 'need to know'.

The high cost of connect-time, coupled to the unfriendliness of the search software, had another result. Any readers who are also Woody Allen fans will remember that sublime moment in *Manhattan* when Allen and Diane Keaton are in the back of a taxi travelling through the neon-lit streets of New York. Allen, gazing at Keaton, murmurs: 'God ... you're so beautiful, I can hardly keep my eyes on the meter.' The experience of using traditional online systems was much the same. The information may well have been the most desirable of prizes but the pressure of connect-time charging meant that users were always aware of a figurative meter ticking up the ultimate bill. In other words, there was no time for gazing, just for grabbing what was needed and getting out. This meant that browsing in online services was unknown. The traditional charging model was not designed to encourage users to maximise their use of services but actually to minimise it. Even today, the paradox of charging for online services on a connect-time basis is that it serves to inhibit online activity rather than promote it.

Given the difficulties of using these traditional forms of online service, it is not surprising that their market was confined to computer users with a strong operational reason for wanting information delivered online. There was certainly no element of pleasure or entertainment – raw need was the driver. Nonetheless, the computerisation of the world's financial markets in the late 1980s gave – as we have seen – a major boost to the industry and together with improvements in telecommunications, more intuitive search engines and more flexible charging models, online database publishing markets have continued to grow at an annual rate of between 9 and 12 per cent, with the lowest level reflecting recession in the world economy at the end of the 1980s. Today professional, corporate and academic online is a substantial and mature industry with about 5,500 databases offered by around 850 online hosts around the world.

But even while the high priced, low volume industry was making its unsteady progress during the 1980s, other operators were creating fledgling services aimed at a radically different market. Companies such as Compu-Serve, Prodigy and America Online had their eyes on a business based on the low priced, high volume economics of the mass market. The belief fuelling the ambitions of these players was that the routine use of computers in academic, professional and corporate sectors would soon migrate to the home and a new generation of consumers would seek interactive information, entertainment and communication over easy-to-use, low priced networks. In the 1980s when these services first launched their offerings, the vision looked a very distant prospect. But, in the early 1990s, the market they had foreseen suddenly emerged. The computerisation of the home, first and at high speed in the United States, and then at a more leisurely pace in Europe, is creating the installed base of computer users that the consumer online services had been hoping to see.

THE MAKING OF A CONSUMER MARKET

It is worth reminding ourselves that the story of the evolution of the online industry exactly parallels the growth and development of CD-ROM publishing. In both cases, their origins and commercial centre of gravity lay in the professional and corporate sector. Their business models – based on low volume, high priced products – were similar. And both have changed out of all recognition in recent years with the rapid emergence of an unprecedented market among home users. Of course, none of this is coincidence nor is it the least surprising. Both online and CD-ROM publishing markets track the use of computers. They have to because computers give access to their offerings and they therefore must follow the patterns of computer usage to find their customers. As the demographics of computer users has widened, so the online and CD-ROM market has grown in line with the change. The reason why major consumer markets for online and CD-ROM have suddenly emerged is because the markets are now tracking the shift of computers into homes. The underlying driver, therefore, has nothing to do with online or CD-ROM in themselves. It is the computerisation of the home with powerful desktop technology that is pulling with it the purchase of CD-ROM drives and modems.

The consumer online market, therefore, is a recent phenomenon even if consumer online offerings have been around since the early 1980s. The only difference between then and now is that the service operators have some customers. Indeed, growth in the market has been phenomenal. Most of the action so far has been in the United States because computerisation of homes has taken place there much more quickly than anywhere else in the world. By the end of 1995, there were around 40 million US homes with at least one PC in them. Out of these, approximately 20 million had PCs with modems making them potential customers of online services. It is important to use the word 'potential' because, as we have already stressed – and this should be engraved on the heart of everyone in the electronic media industry – the possession of technology does not necessarily imply its use. In 1994, for example, a survey of PC homes with modems in the United States showed that 32 per cent of the modems had never been connected to a telephone line. In other words, ownership of modems, while obviously necessary to the growth of the consumer online market, is not enough to guarantee that growth. Consumers need both the technology and the motivation to use the technology. In the case of online networks, this means not only modems but also a perception that online services are worth using.

This is a key area for anyone trying to predict growth patterns to consider. We have spent years in the digital media industry struggling with various statistics purportedly indicating the rise of installed bases of hardware. The logic was obvious. The rise in the numbers of CD-ROM drives and modems being purchased indicated the rise in the number of CD-ROM drives and modems being used. This was a fair assumption so long as the equipment was relatively costly and purchased as add-ons to computers. Today, the hardware is cheap and is increasingly sold integrated with PCs as part of a routine value package. In other words, PC buyers are getting CD-ROM drives and modems whether or not they particularly want them. Many, of course, may use them avidly, extensively and for ever. Others may try a CD-ROM title or two or may accept an online service's promotional offer of some free connect-time but then dismiss either or both as unsatisfactory. The underlying market reality, therefore, is that while CD-ROM and online publishing track the demographics of the PC market, the link between the installed base of hardware and a revenue-generating market is weakening. We can no longer rely on the traditional assumption that another modem sold means another long-term customer for online services. The onus is on industry players to commercialise the installed base. They cannot assume that the installed base will come to them.

CONSUMER ONLINE NETWORKS

We will look first in this section at the rise of proprietary online services, leaving the Internet's remarkable growth in use and influence until later. In reality, the two strands are closely intertwined and the evolution of proprietary services has in recent months and years been largely shaped by the development of Internet services and the extraordinary growth in their use by all kinds of online customers. Indeed, the concept of a network that is, in the traditional sense, proprietary may soon vanish altogether.

To understand the impact of the Internet on the proprietary industry, we need to step back to the time a few years ago when the Internet was simply not an issue in consumer markets. In the early 1990s, the few networks designed for consumers were just beginning to feel the impact of an emerging market-place. At the end of 1993, the total number of subscribers to consumer online services was around 3 million, almost all in the United States. Two years later, the number had grown to around 10 million. The rapid growth brought both joys and anguish. The proprietary networks suddenly had customers and their huge infrastructure, content and marketing investments could at last be clawed back. But with customers came competition and an increasingly savage battle for market share. The battle – fought almost exclusively in the United States – has resolved itself into fierce competition between the three major players: CompuServe, the only one with a long-standing presence outside the US market, America Online (AOL), the fastest growing of the three, and the IBM/Sears joint venture, Prodigy, arguably the weakest of the main contenders. The ferocity of the competition was fuelled by a single disquieting factor. As the numbers of subscribers grew, it became increasingly evident that consumers using online services were not easily persuaded to spend money on those services beyond the initial subscription. To understand the implications of this we need to examine the basic business model on which all the main services are based.

Consumer online services have a very simple and persuasive proposition for subscribers. They offer for a modest monthly payment – typically a few dollars – access to a 'warehouse' of content and service offerings. CompuServe, for example, has over 3,000 products on the shelves of its warehouse and rightly argues that amongst such a vast selection there must surely be something to attract everyone. This tells us something important about subscribers to these kinds of services. They form a potentially large but very unfocused constituency. No single thread of interest or common concern has drawn them together, merely the attraction of a low cost key to a treasure house of information, entertainment and communications.

The implication of this proposition is that the networks have to attract very large numbers of subscribers to make their business model work. In other words, the approach is to build a high volume of users, each spending relatively small amounts. But networks ardently hope to be able to increase those relatively small amounts by getting consumers to spend money beyond their basic monthly subscriptions. While the subscription buys the key to the door, users generally only get a few hours of free connect-time – currently varying between five and ten hours per month – and if they remain online longer they are billed at a modest rate per hour. Additionally, not all the products and services in the warehouse are free. Many of them may be considered premium offerings, attracting an additional charge for use, based either on connect-time or a flat fee. Some genres of services, of course, are always free. For example, transactional services such as home shopping or travel reservations are free to users – who could imagine charging a fee allowing entry to a shop? – with networks getting a commission on the value of transactions conducted by their subscribers. Taken together, therefore, consumer networks aim to generate enough revenue from all these sources to cover their continuing investment in computing and telecommunications infrastructure, marketing and content.

The cost of content, of course, varies enormously but the key point to appreciate about network operators is that traditionally they have owned none themselves. In other words, all the content offered from their warehouses is licensed from content owners. We will look at the basis of these licences shortly but for now it is important to understand that the networks are merely packagers of content acquired from third parties. As packagers, their decisions about what to license and how to deploy services based on what they license, crucially distinguishes them from their competitors and ultimately determines whether or not they attract and retain customers.

We now need to return to the realities of the market-place. We have outlined the way that consumer networks attempt to derive revenue from their subscribers. Their objective is to build a large constituency, retain and grow it and ultimately commercialise it by generating revenue from its use of online services. The reality has been a shattering blow. It is still not entirely clear what consumers like doing online but it is apparent what they do not like doing. Sadly for the online companies, they do not like spending money. In other words, typical consumers pay their subscriptions and then use no more than the 'free' connect-time included each month. They tend to avoid premium services and use instead the free services such as electronic mail and communications-based offerings such as forums and real-time chat areas. The position is easily confirmed. Just look at the revenues that consumer online services generate compared to the average number of subscribers they have. The arithmetic is changing fast now that access to the Internet has become a part of their offerings but, on the whole, in 1995 at least the total revenues of the companies could be roughly calculated by multiplying their average number of subscribers by the average cost of subscribing to the service.

This has one very powerful message for the big players among the proprietary online services. They have a vital battle to fight to gain as much market share as possible. The only way they can build their revenues – at least, based on the traditional charging model – is to increase the raw number of their subscribers. On the basis of their experience, it does not seem to matter who their subscribers are – there is no one demographic group that appears to be prepared to spend more than another – so sheer quantity is the issue. The result has been two-fold. First, the majors have launched aggressive and sustained marketing campaigns. Vast numbers of floppy disks are being given away embodying access software for their networks combined with trial offers providing a free access for limited periods. Second, the fierce competition has driven down monthly subscription and additional connect-time charges. In an increasingly vicious spiral, this has in turn served to intensify the need to win even more subscribers.

A key weapon in this competitive free-for-all is content and, in particular, strongly branded content. We need, therefore, to consider how the network operators are managing the acquisition and deployment of content in order to attract and retain customers. Traditionally, the proposition for content companies has not been especially appealing. The arrangement was known as the '80:20' deal meaning that the network licensing the content retained 80 per cent of all revenue generated through use of the content, leaving 20 per cent for the content owners. In practice, this percentage break varied around 15–30 per cent going to providers of content, depending on how badly the network wanted the particular content concerned. A strongly branded product such as a bestselling magazine or globally acclaimed news service might be so desirable that networks would pay up to 50 per cent plus a substantial advance. In cases where the content was not going to become a premium offering and would, therefore, not generate income directly from network use, a fee was negotiated, the size of the amount again depending on the desirability of the content.

But the split of the revenue or the fee paid was only one aspect of the overall deal. Traditionally, networks would drive a hard bargain on payment and then force through other conditions. Usually, they would require partial or complete exclusivity from the content owner. They would retain complete control over the design of the service created using the content and determine its pricing. Apart from any other consideration, this means that strongly branded content would find the look and feel of its branding subsumed by the network's branding. Whoever you were in the real world and however well known you were for being it, on the networks you became firmly a CompuServe, AOL or Prodigy offering with your branding only deployed to support theirs. Lastly, network operators are able to track in detail what their individual subscribers do when they access services but all these valuable consumer data would be retained by the network. Content companies would merely receive a bald statement of usage each month with no indication even of who generated the usage let alone what they did while accessing the service. In other words, the network owned the customers and the content companies hosted on the network could gain no access to them.

This simplifies what has in reality been a much more complex picture. In practice, there are many other potential ingredients in a deal and much room for negotiation between the parties. But the elements outlined above demonstrate a single, unquestionable fact. The traditional deal between consumer online companies and content owners was always strongly weighted in favour of the online companies. Why then did content consent to these unattractive terms? The answer is telling because it reminds us of a fast disappearing attitude in the world of content. The reason that content did the deals was because the online companies were the only show in town and content had no intention or possibility of exploiting its assets independently. At the time these deals were commonplace, content was entirely dedicated to its traditional channels of delivery. The only exception was some experimentation with CD-ROM publishing. But there were few content companies who saw a future in which they might seek to leverage their assets across a wide range of electronic platforms and channels of delivery. Content still saw itself in its traditional niches dedicated to its usual forms of product and delivery mechanism. The idea, for example, that a book publisher might extend its core business by developing its own online service was a sheer flight of fancy. The possibility of getting its content hosted online – however miserly the terms – was therefore an added value opportunity and any revenue generated was a bonus.

Three important factors have combined to reshape this traditional position and have served to redefine the relationship between content and proprietary networks. First, competition has forced online players to bid increasingly highly for the most valued content assets. In 1995, for example, some of Time Inc.'s flagship magazines were prised away from AOL by CompuServe with an upfront payment well into seven figures. Second, content is now increasingly aware that markets are emerging rapidly for digital media and that content interpreted appropriately for such media will determine commercial success. Content companies, therefore, are growing acutely aware that as information, entertainment and education markets increasingly go digital, their conventional media assets are acquiring an additional and growing potential value. Third, content now has somewhere else to go and, for the first time, can seriously contemplate setting up its own online initiatives cheaply, quickly and globally. In other words, the rise of the non-proprietary Internet has provided content owners with an unprecedented opportunity to find autonomy in online publishing without the need for investing huge sums in infrastructure and software.

All these factors have forced great change upon the business practices of the proprietary majors. In terms of their relationships with content companies, the old '80:20' arrangement has been widely revised to become a '20:80' deal, advantage now having swung to favour content. And exclusivity is rarely requested, except when extremely high fees or royalties are paid. The only exception among the major players to this shift in emphasis is AOL, which retains its tough 80:20 policy. Tellingly, the reason for this is that AOL is the least dependent of all the proprietaries on content, favouring instead communications-based services such as forums, conferences and chat areas – the kinds of online experiences which consumers seem to relish most.

Something of a wild card also driving change in the relationships between content and online service operators has been the emergence of two new online platforms. The first, known as Interchange, was created by the online division of Ziff Davis and was subsequently acquired by AT & T as part of the break-up of the Ziff Davis publishing empire at the end of 1994. The second was the new proprietary network created by the Microsoft Corporation and today known widely as MSN (standing for the Microsoft Network). AT & T's Interchange is a publishing platform, a software structure that can, in principle, be utilised by different proprietary players. In practice, AT & T expect to commercialise it themselves in the United States, probably delivering a business-oriented service. In Europe, it was widely expected that a company called Europe Online would deploy Interchange as the basis of a new consumer service. It has since changed its strategy and Interchange is beginning to look like an answer in search of a question. The MSN by contrast is a full consumer online venture and is never likely to be utilised by anyone other than its creators. Indeed, not only is it highly proprietary but also it has been promoted in an intensely proprietary manner. Launched at the same time as Microsoft's important new operating system, Windows 95, in August 1995, access to MSN was embedded in the Windows software. This meant that every new user of Windows 95 would need only to click an icon on their Windows worktop to enter and try out the online service. Since the number of Windows 95 users could grow to tens of millions within a few years, Microsoft's marketing ploy was and is a powerful one – so powerful that it has attracted the eye of the anti-competition regulators in the United States together with the anger of other competitors in the online market. Pressure may now ease, however, since – as we will see when we consider the impact of the Internet more generally on proprietary services – Microsoft, only months after launching the network, is now completely rethinking it, abandoning the original proprietary model and using MSN instead as an influential access point for the subset of the Internet known as the World Wide Web.

Despite their dissimilarities in design and commercial prospects, the reason why we should bracket together the Interchange and MSN as originally conceived is because they present a radically different proposition for both content companies seeking to be hosted online and for consumers seeking to find an online service that both holds their attention and offers an attractive charging model. Unlike the online services which preceded them Interchange and MSN both offer a high degree of autonomy for content companies. To examine this, we will concentrate on Microsoft's original plan for MSN since Interchange is anyway looking increasingly like a lame duck, unlikely to have much future impact on the market.

MSN's original proposition for content companies is interesting because it not only offers a financial deal along the lines of the 20:80 arrangements increasingly becoming current but also allows content companies to build and operate their own sites on the MSN. Using Microsoft's own development tools, contributors to MSN can design the appearance and interactivities of their offerings – so ensuring that their visual brandings are preserved – and control the pricing of their services. This means that MSN is positioning itself not as the ruler of the network, only as the reliable owner of a huge virtual mall. Using this analogy, MSN is the landlord who makes sure the mall is heated, lighted, well signposted and clean (no bugs!) and who does his best to attract and direct visitors to the various stores located in the mall. The content companies pay their rent to MSN and can then design and set up their own shopfronts, determine what goods they will put on their shelves and how they wish to price them. MSN also deals with all billing and customer management so the payments by users for services purchased are always assured through MSN's secure, centralised procedures. Perhaps most crucially of all, MSN is ready to share information about the demographics of users of the mall and will allow shop owners to access the names of visitors to their stores and to track their activities while inside. This is not perfect since MSN still retains a strong proprietary interest in the data and will not reveal the details of the gross, mall-wide data. However, it is a vast improvement over the usual practice of online operators keeping the data entirely for themselves.

The proposition for MSN subscribers looks less appealing. The underlying concept is to offer a pay-as-you-go experience. Monthly subscriptions to MSN are very modest – just enough to pay for the upkeep of the mall – and charging thereafter depends on the sites within MSN that are visited and the charging policy determined by each site owner. This à la carte approach to an online service appears to make good sense. After all, subscribers can decide for themselves what they buy and the network as a whole does not have to pass on the cost of maintaining a huge body of licensed content via high monthly subscriptions. The flaw in the logic is obvious. First, à la carte is fine until the bill comes in. Subscribers may find it all too easy to meander around sites buying piecemeal here and there without realising how much money they are spending when it is finally aggregated into a single bill. Second, the low cost of entry to MSN no longer looks especially attractive. Competitive pressure has already driven down the entry cost of accessing the traditional proprietaries. Moreover, those established players show up the weakness of the à la carte model. As efficient packagers of content, their proposition cannot be bettered. Low cost entry into an established body of products or services which are – on the whole – freely available to subscribers.

The key point here is not merely a matter of competitive analysis – the issue of whether MSN will succeed against established players – but the continuing powerful role of information intermediaries in online publishing. The traditional online companies are aggregators of both content and consumers. In this sense they act as powerful go-betweens, mediating the relationship of content and its market. They offer content companies access (at a price) to their powerful, multimillion-strong constituencies and they offer their constituencies low cost access to a distinctive bouquet of content. When we come to examine the role of content on the Internet, we will return to the importance of intermediaries because their strategic influence lies at the heart of successfully commercialising online markets.

CONSUMER ONLINE SERVICES IN EUROPE

Although the underlying principles apply anywhere, many of the commercial activities and market developments we have discussed have been taking place in the United States. And, although we have emphasised that networks do not recognise national boundaries, they are sensitive to market demand. Europe, therefore, has been an arena distinct from the US consumer online market and needs to be examined separately. We will not attempt detailed analysis of European developments – such coverage would be beyond the scope of this book – but it is important at least to examine some of the main themes that are emerging and touch on the principal initiatives that are emerging.

Although the penetration of PCs into European homes has leaped in recent years, the growth of the installed base of modems has been modest. This is not surprising since there has been little infrastructure of consumer online services – outside the business and professional sectors – to attract and drive usage. The only such service with a broadly based offering has been CompuServe which, though based in the United States, has systematically built an infrastructure of points of presence and subsidiary companies in many parts of the world. In Europe – where it began marketing its service in 1989 – it has today about 45 points of presence. Its only two success stories so far, however, have been the UK and Germany and even here penetrations have been modest. At the end of 1994, for example, CompuServe's European subscribers numbered around 200,000 compared to its US customer base of around 2 million. In 1995, it has greatly increased the number of its European subscribers but still has fewer than 500,000 compared to about 3 million in the United States. These figures are approximate but give a strong sense of the real centres of gravity of the market-place.

But as the computerisation of the home proceeds and as interest builds in the United States in online markets, a range of European initiatives are emerging, targeting the consumer market in the belief, no doubt, that 'if we build it, they will come'. At the time of writing, for example, Olivetti-Telemedia – the new media arm of the Italian-based computer hardware and communications company Olivetti – has been the main investor in two online ventures: Italia Online in Italy and UK Online (UKOL) in Britain. Both services are strictly national initiatives with no pan-European ambitions. Elsewhere, pan-European objectives are firmly a part of the recent alliance between America Online and European media giant Bertelsmann. The first fruits of this alliance, announced early in 1995 and now branded AOL Europe, has been the launch of a new German online service with French, British and other national roll-outs planned for 1996 and 1997. Similarly, Europe Online – a Luxembourg-based start-up with backing from Burda in Germany and Pearson in the UK – has a strong pan-European agenda although, at the time of writing, it is rapidly shifting its strategy towards the Internet and is seemingly struggling to gain the kind of content base that will distinguish its offering to the market. Meantime, despite its dramatic change of strategy at the end of 1995, Microsoft's

MSN – conceived ultimately as a global service with points of presence all over the world – is also being strongly promoted in Europe and will become increasingly significant as the preferred portal to the Internet as Windows 95 – with which MSN access is bundled – becomes more popular with European PC users.

Although, as we have noted, there have been few broadly based online services in Europe in the past, these relatively new developments are being delivered alongside some existing infrastructures. We mentioned Compu-Serve's existing presence in Europe as if it was the only significant service but we should not forget that videotex services, particularly in France and Germany, while not fully fledged online services, nonetheless have traditionally provided users with an extensive, broadly based 'near online' experience.

In France, for example, France Telecom has been offering its Teletel service since 1981, available largely through Minitel terminals which were given away in millions to kick start the viability of the underlying service. This radical strategy has borne fruit with over 6.5 million terminals now installed serving up to 20 million regular users of the service. Although about half of all usage is business related, France Telecom believes that over one-third of all French homes have a Minitel terminal. Turnover for France Telecom in 1994 from Minitel business was over £1.3 billion with the most common use being to check telephone numbers. Indeed, Minitel – as it is commonly known – was originally positioned as the answer to printed phone directories which were largely withdrawn when the service was first launched. Other major uses today include business-to-business services, home banking and chat services – particularly *les messageries roses* (literally 'pink mailboxes') which offer the chance to enjoy what are euphemistically called 'adult' communications services (when in reality that is the last thing they are!).

Despite its success, however, growth in Minitel has petered out. The installed base is not growing significantly and although the use of the service still generates huge revenues, France Telecom is urgently trying to shift its emphasis away from the fairly primitive, low-resolution experience it gives now to a more sophisticated PC-based environment. As a part of this strategy, France Telecom is also actively developing modern new online services as France-en-Ligne – intended to shift the Minitel market into a mainstream online market – and Wanadoo, a consumer entertainment service created through a joint venture with the French publishing giant, Havas.

In Germany, the national telecommunications company is also a major player in online services. Originally called Datex-J, Deutsche Telekom's videotex service has been offering page-based online information for business users and consumers since the mid-1980s. In recent years, Deutsche Telekom has been upgrading and modernising the service and successfully migrating new subscribers towards accessing it via PCs rather than videotex terminals. Subscriber growth has been rapid with over a million by the end of 1995, almost twice the number using the service in 1993.

We will not examine either of these important services in detail. The key point about them, however, is that they indicate how different the commercial climate is for the emergence of online services in Europe from the United States. Whatever we think of France Telecom's or Deutsche Telekom's current offerings, the fact that two state telecommunications companies – both with immense political clout – have a major grip over two of Europe's most important markets is a major complicating factor for independent online initiatives. Indeed, it is one of the reasons why so little has happened so far in Europe and why newly spawned initiatives – such as the AOL Europe or Europe Online initiatives – have a much greater level of competitive pressure to cope with than the otherwise somewhat blank European online scene would suggest.

Europe is also distinct from the United States for a related but much more prosaic reason. Local telephony in the States is largely free, meaning that most online connections do not incur the cost of a local phone call. In Europe, current regulatory restrictions prevent most telecommunications companies from offering a free local service and – for now, at least – going online will mean paying both online service providers and the telephone companies. This is not a killer for online growth but it will plainly inhibit growth. For this and many other reasons, Europe must be seen as a distinct arena for online (and offline) developments and while analysis of the US industry is important to indicate the processes of change which will ultimate shape market opportunities in Europe, we have to remember that the European metabolism is different. The pace and character of change may be broadly based on US indicators but those indicators need careful reinterpretation before they can be applied to Europe with any accuracy.

There is one thing we have learned very clearly from the pioneering quality of the US market which applies unconditionally to European developments. The proprietary networks which have both suffered and enjoyed such huge growth in recent years have all run into the same wall. The message of their experience is that the real future of online services is dominated not by narrow proprietary interests but by the wide open spaces of the Internet.

THE INTERNET

The history of the Internet is well documented elsewhere and we will concentrate here only on establishing the main themes. To some extent, because it is impossible to discuss the background of online markets without immediately referring to the Internet, we have already begun to explore these themes above. But, at the risk of being repetitious, we will reprise some of this material in order to make the story of the growth of the Internet clearer and more accessible.

The Internet has been the subject of immense hype, particularly by the popular press. There are even some influential thinkers – such as Professor Nicholas Negroponte of the Massachusetts Institute of Technology Media Lab – who believe that the hype is actually an understatement of the likely impact of the Internet on human lives. Despite all the hype, however, and – more importantly – the concrete indications, there remains a body of critics who argue that – as a commercial environment – the Internet simply does not work. Plenty of detractors who claim it is too slow, too unfriendly, too insecure, too unregulated and too light on bandwidth ever to deliver the global trading space which many are trying to create. There are good reasons for these criticisms but they all focus on a single fact which stems from the Internet's origins. The Internet was designed for a purpose that had little to do with commerce and the problems we are experiencing trying to use the Internet for trade is simply the result of us trying – necessarily – to make it do something for which it was never designed.

When the Internet was built in the mid-1970s, it was conceived as a small but crucial project in the US Department of Defense Advanced Research Projects Agency (ARPA). The idea was to create a communications system able to link a variety of different computers which would continue working even in the event of a nuclear war. Although under the auspices of ARPA, the project originally involved several US government research agencies and a number of universities. By 1978, the so-called Kahn-Cerf protocols (named after their inventors) had been developed to control communications over a prototype network. These quickly evolved into the Internet protocols (IP or transmission control protocol TCP/IP) which are today in use in millions of host computers all over the world.

The original focused aim of the protocols was soon almost forgotten as the academic and research communities, first in the United States, and then more globally, began to develop the original protocols into a full suite which offered a range of possible applications. These included file transfer protocol (FTP), which allows the transfer of computer files across the network, Telnet, which effectively makes a remote computer behave as if it was connected to the local network of a distant host, and electronic mail, which is today still the most extensively used function of the Internet. The communities of academics and researchers who built the foundations of the Internet, therefore, were, and remain today, fluent computer users. Most had already experienced the power of networking their computers on a local area basis within their own institutions and campuses but were attracted by the possibility of exchanging computer-held ideas and information over much greater distances. In other words, these communities physically located at great distances from one another wanted to talk to one another – in the most general sense – and wanted to do so electronically. The urge to link locally operated networks was the driver for the mutual development of the software protocols which, when shared among the different locations, allowed intercommunication. These protocols, therefore, effectively define what we today call the Internet – a vast, expanding global network of interconnecting computer networks.

As we noted earlier, the important thing about the Internet's protocols was – and is today – the fact that they were open to all users. They were not owned by any single entity and being non-proprietary were therefore available to anyone who could get hold of a copy and had the computer knowledge to make them work. There was, of course, one other thing they needed: access to the physical network which carried the traffic of the Internet.

Today, of course, hundreds of companies are rapidly getting rich by all being able to offer a package consisting of the free-to-anybody protocols that make computers talk the lingo of the Internet together with access – preferably fast access – into the Internet itself. But the reason there is now such a business is based on more than the fact that the underlying software that makes the Internet run is not proprietary. It is based, more importantly, in an explosion of use and a huge shift in the demographics of those who can now get benefits from touring the byways and thoroughfares of what is rapidly becoming the world's first incarnation of the long-dreamed-of information superhighway.

THE RISE AND RISE OF THE INTERNET

To understand the rise of the Internet we need to start with the origins we have just outlined. The key point about those origins – as we discussed earlier – is that they lay in the hands of individuals who had a deep understanding of computers. In other words, the Internet is historically an environment designed by computer users for computer users. This means that for 'ordinary' human beings – those who understand (and want to understand) little about computers and struggle to make them do something useful – the Internet has long been a deeply unfriendly and unintelligible place, a kind of technological 'no-go' area. This, of course, did not matter much because the Internet did the job it was designed for very well and those for whom it was designed knew its language and could use it for their desired ends with little or no difficulty. Even in this polarised state, however, the Internet was growing rapidly. Starting as the enthusiasm of a small group of US engineers and scientists – supported financially by the US government – the attractions of the Internet quickly fired global interest. Beyond the US academic and research networks which were first to be connected, thousands more networks all over the world gained access to the Internet and began sharing in and adding to the expanding community of users. To get some idea of the speed of growth consider these statistics from the Internet Society. In the early 1980s, the number of host computers connected numbered in the low hundreds. By 1988, the number was 33,000. By 1992, the year immediately before the Internet was opened to a much wider community, the host count had reached just under 1 million! It was impossible to determine how many individuals were using the Internet because, while it was possible to assess the number of networks interconnected, no one could know how many individuals made use of their Internet links, particularly since most networks were based on university or institutional campus where students, staff and researchers could make largely unrecorded use of the systems whenever they chose. All that was clear was that by the early 1990s, the users were numbered in millions and were growing daily.

All of this growth was reflecting enthusiasm for what the Internet was when it was created. New applications were being found by individuals all the time – the Usenet discussion groups which created the first interest-centred virtual communities, for example – so the Internet was evolving. But its centre of gravity lay with the computer-literate community of academics, researchers and students for whom it was originally designed. In 1993, however, a dramatic change took place which has transformed the world of information and media for ever.

The starting point of the revolution is mundane. A group of physicists based at the Geneva high energy research centre, CERN, led by Tim Berners-Lee, were interested in extending the functionality of the Internet. In particular, they were seeking a way of introducing hypertext linking to documents held on Internet servers so that they could follow a trail of interest among research reports, figuratively clicking on a word and being taken directly to another part of the same document or to another relevant document on a completely different server system. The team achieved this by creating a new Internet protocol called hypertext transfer protocol (HTTP) based on inserting special codes – derived from a new mark-up language they devised called hypertext markup language (HTML) – into electronic documents which would create the hypertext links they were after. In practice, the system ascribed a unique address to documents and pages within documents, held on servers. These addresses were called universal resource locators (URLs). When a code was activated, it automatically pointed the user at the URL of the related information, wherever it was physically located. Using the system, it was possible to 'jump' from page to page, document to document, server to server, creating a kind of web of interconnectivity spanning the Internet. Berners-Lee and his colleagues struck on a name for their invention which summed it up perfectly. They called it the World Wide Web.

The underlying technology of the Web is conceptually simple. A computer acting as an Internet server is turned into a site on the Web by running some software on the server that enables it to talk the language of HTTP. Once it is talking that language, it can offer documents marked up with HTML codes and allow users to link from other servers to the documents or to use the documents as jumping off points to other sites on the Web.

THE WORLD WIDE WEB

The creation of the Web was not a revolution in itself, only the catalyst of revolution. Despite the fact that it was simple in concept, the Web in its early days was as unfriendly and complex to use as the Internet had always been. This is not surprising. It had – like the Internet – been created by computer professionals for other computer professionals. In other words, if you happened to be an elementary particle physicist, you could manipulate the language of HTTP and navigate the Web with ease. Ordinary information seekers would find the Unix-based command language a fearsome obstacle. Of course, navigating the Web in the days immediately following its invention was a relatively short journey. In June 1993, for example, a few months after Berners-Lee and his team had released details of HTTP and HTML, there were just 50 Web sites in existence. As this book is written in the spring of 1996, there are already over 100,000 sites and some believe there are many more – indeed, the number is growing so fast, it is impossible to keep track of new sites as they emerge.

What has caused this explosion? Certainly not the Web's popularity among academics and researchers – although their use of it has expanded dramatically. Instead it has been the sudden appearance of ordinary computer users in their millions with access both to the Internet in general and to the Web in particular. The Web has been tamed and democratised by a single key invention – the creation of an easy-to-use, graphical point and click window through which anyone can navigate and view the Web. The window is a specialised form of software which is run on client computers to provide an instant interface for the Web. The generic name for the software sums up its use. It is known as a Web browser.

The first browser to emerge appeared in the autumn of 1993, about six months after Berners-Lee published the foundations on which the Web could be built. Called Mosaic, the software was authored by a team of brilliant young programmers led by Marc Andreeson working at the National Center for Supercomputing Applications (NCSA), a department of the University of Illinois headquartered in Chicago. Its impact was instantaneous – largely because Andreeson and his team made it freely available via the Internet. Initially, thousands of students and academics downloaded the software via their campus Internet connections and began to surf the fledgling Web. As news of its ease of use spread, the Internet, for the first time, became an interesting proposition for a more general audience of computer users. As the audience grew in numbers and broadened in its demographic, increasing numbers of Web sites emerged. And they were not only focused on technical subjects such as elementary particle physics. Campus Internet servers quickly became hosts to a wide range of interest-based Web sites covering every imaginable enthusiasm. Web evangelists publicised the new sites by word of mouth and through specialist newsletters. The word of the Web spread like wildfire and ignited a major new industry. Suddenly, through the arrival of a form of software which turned the Internet from a hostile to a friendly place, millions of people wanted to get wired. Companies offering dial-up access sprang up overnight, providing low cost subscriptions that gave both admission via fast leased connections and the software needed to enjoy the fruits of the Internet – electronic mail, access to Internet discussion groups, the ability to download software from distant hosts and, of course, a Web browser to allow users to wander the fast expanding landscape of cyberspace.

This process of democratisation – the conversion of net users from a select elite of computer literate boffins and enthusiasts to ordinary consumers hungry for information, entertainment and communications – took place with breathtaking speed. From early 1993 to early 1996, the number of consumers with dial-up access from their homes grew from zero to about 10 million worldwide. Berners-Lee's World Wide Web was the catalyst and Mosaic was the key ingredient that triggered revolution. But Mosaic was merely a jumping off point for the creation of really effective and powerful browsing technology. While the NCSA was giving away its fledgling – and often unstable – software, commercial software companies were increasingly interested in licensing it and improving it for widespread use. Licensing deals were concluded between the Trustees of the University of Illinois and such companies as Spyglass and Spry, who immediately began making Mosaic more robust and reliable. Elsewhere, however, commercial forces were gathering to sweep aside the link with NCSA's Mosaic and build an independent browsing technology. In fact the link with the NCSA remained but merely became less formal. In mid-1994, Jim Clark, founder and former CEO of computer hardware company Silicon Graphics, created a new organisation called Mosaic Communications. To do it he did not buy the Mosaic software from NCSA but, instead, raided the NCSA for all its key programming staff. Most importantly, Clark tempted Andreeson away and with him came most of his team. With the creators of the original Mosaic successfully employed, Clark set about building a new form of Mosaic working from the ground up. The result was today's best known and most widely used browser, Netscape Navigator. All the University of Illinois could do about the perfectly legitimate and shrewd-minded hijack was to force Clark to change the name of his company from Mosaic to Netscape Communications.

Clark began giving away Netscape Navigator from his company's Web site in autumn 1994. By spring the following year, more than 6 million people had downloaded the software and Netscape was well on its way to becoming the de facto standard for browsing the Web. Clark was not giving his software away as an act of altruism. His agenda was simple. Give away the software and create a huge market of users dependent on your free product. Then start charging modestly for upgrades of the product. But, more importantly, sell Web site operators server software (for thousands of dollars) which complements the features of the Netscape browser. Although all HTTP-compliant browsers could access all Web sites, whatever flavour of Web software they were running, it was possible to add proprietary features by expanding upon and redeveloping the underlying HTTP mark-up language. This was the golden opportunity that Clark spotted and Netscape grasped. Having established an installed base of millions of users within months, Clark's proposition for the increasing number of commercial organisations wanting to build Web sites was almost irresistible: use Netscape's server software and address a vast population of browser users with the fullest possible range of Netscape features – including the ability to make secure transmissions of data between client and server, something that was possible only when a Netscape browser links to a server running Netscape software.

COMMERCIALISING THE WEB

The explosion in the use of the Web was startling and spectacular. But while commentators became obsessed with the sheer speed and scale of the development, commercial forces were beginning to see the presence of the Web as a stepping stone to a major new commercial opportunity. Initially, the expanding number of sites merely reflected the individual enthusiasms of Web users, particularly those with easy access to server infrastructure in research institutions and university campuses. But by early 1994, the first commercial sites began to emerge. Within a year, commercial sites blossomed as the most active sector of Web development. The types of sites were immensely varied. Large companies created sites to wave their corporate flags. Media companies went online to promote their latest movies, record albums or computer games. Newspapers set up online counterparts. Magazine companies did the same. Retailers and merchants of different kinds began exploring the possibilities of electronic shopping. The range of activity is too wide to summarise. But the basic trend was clear. The newly democratised Web was suddenly perceived as a vast new market-place where products and services could be commercialised instantly and internationally. Most intriguing of all, it seemed as if all you needed to grab a slice of the action was a fast PC and an Internet connection. Setting up shop in cyberspace looked like a cheap and easy thing to do. Accordingly everyone stampeded towards what looked at the outset like a golden opportunity, a licence to print money.

The reality has been quite different and while commentators like Negroponte may argue that the hype does not even begin to express the true magnitude of the impact of the Web, there is a serious issue of timescale to address. The pace of recent developments has been so rapid that it is tempting to think that the Web in particular and the Internet in general will soon become a mature environment for doing business. But the truth is that we are still in the first day of school. We not only have to master and improve the technologies underpinning the Internet to make it into a friendly, secure and pervasive environment but also need to build effective, new business models to create stable businesses that will prosper and flourish long term.

CHAPTER 6

WEB COMMERCE

In chapter 5 we looked at the rise of proprietary consumer networks – a phenomenon driven by the rapid computerisation of US and European homes – and the emergence of the Internet as a mainstream online environment. In this chapter, we will focus on the single most important subset of the Internet for commercial activity – the World Wide Web. We will examine in particular the main basis for commercialising the Web and outline the key means of generating revenue from Web sites. Through examining its commercialisation, we will also be able to make sense of its devastating impact on the traditional business model of proprietary networks.

THE WEB CONSUMER

We have already gained a sense of how quickly the Web has grown in size and significance. There are many wild estimates of how many new sites are appearing. Some claim they double every few months while others struggle with the maths and come up with at least one site every minute. The truth is, no one really knows how quickly the Web is growing. The only certainty is that it is growing fast. As this book is printed, the likely number of sites is probably around 200,000 and may double by the time it is in the hands of its first readers. Anyone can come up with numbers but it is really a matter of educated guesswork.

More solid numbers are available for the other end of the equation. There are plenty of sites: no doubt about it. But how many consumers are actually using the Web? What is the audience for this massive treasure house of online experiences? A US survey conducted by FIND/SVP in late 1995 gives at least part of the answer. It revealed 9.5 million Internet users in the United States of which 7.5 million had access to the Web. Of those using the Web, 4 million (fully 53 per cent of the total) began using it in 1995. Of the newcomers, 48 per cent were using the Web exclusively from home. Out of all US Internet users, only 27 per cent were using it via a server in an academic institution, a figure that would have been closer to 100 per cent only two years earlier. Servers in business locations accounted for 28 per cent, indicating the rapid moves that corporations are making to embrace the Internet.

The real surprise in the figures came when the researchers analysed the proportion of Internet users gaining access from specialist Internet service providers (ISPs), companies that had originally ridden high on the Internet boom and had been the main source of Internet provision since the crucial emergence of the first Web browsers. The results showed a significant decline in the influence of smaller ISPs and a rapid rise in the number of people accessing the Internet via proprietary networks. Why is this so remarkable? The proprietary networks had really woken up to the existence of the Internet only in late 1994 and had begun to use their own infrastructure to offer their subscribers Internet access by early 1995. This emphasises the speed with which proprietary networks have taken off as an important source of access to the Internet, driving home the message that the vast majority of newcomers to the Web were the kind of people who might subscribe to populist networks such as AOL or Prodigy and, to a lesser extent, CompuServe – in other words: mainstream consumers. The figures also tell an important story about the remarkable transformation that has taken place in the proprietary network's proposition to its customers. Without exception, proprietary consumer networks have reshaped their business models so that they are now almost exclusively defined by the influence of the Internet in general and the Web in particular.

SURFING THE WEB

There used to be a time when nets were used for fishing, getting wired was an activity strictly for electricians and surfing was a watersport. Today, the vocabulary has assumed a different set of meanings. The particular expression 'surfing the Web' has, in only a matter of months, become one of the worst clichés of the digital world. It was meant to imply a kind of carefree voyage of discovery which users of the Web embarked upon with every click of the mouse. Hyperlink after hyperlink would carry them through an infinite number of pathways in cyberspace. They would pause here and there to take a closer look at one offering or another but the journey was the thing: a ceaseless roaming in search of – second worst cliché – the 'coolest site' on the Web.

Regular users of the Web quickly appreciate that aimless wanderings are ultimately too boring and futile for anyone to tolerate for long. The reality of Web surfing is that surfers need to be directed, they yearn for navigational aids. In the same US Internet survey we quoted above, researchers confirmed with a single finding the fact that underpins almost every strategy for successfully commercialising the Web. Out of all the millions using the Web with its (possibly) hundreds of thousands of sites, 60 per cent of users visit fewer than ten sites on a regular basis! In other words, Web surfing is not an arbitrary wandering, a voyage of discovery. Web users find the sites they like and stick to them. If they expand the number of sites they visit regularly they do so by being directed from a site they already know, enjoy and trust. What this means is vital for Web publishing. It means that it is possible to arbitrate how people use the Web, to influence what they do and where they go. Despite the independence that the structure of the Web confers, its vastness and complexity demands the simplifying effect of navigational beacons, pointers to what is the best, most interesting and most relevant to our needs.

The idea of arbitration – expressed in different ways – is essential to strategic power over the Web and all its commercial potential. Before we look at how this works for site owners, let us consider first some models for gatekeeping the Web which illustrate the potential for finding different forms of influence.

The most obvious example of a gatekeeping play is Netscape Communication's effort to turn its Web browser, Netscape Navigator, into a universal standard and to link this with a grip on Web server supply. Although we have covered much of this ground in chapter 5, we will reprise the main ideas in this new context. Netscape, as we saw, is the brainchild of Jim Clark, former CEO of Silicon Graphics. Clark was one of the first to spot the potential of the NCSA's Mosaic browser for revolutionising global access to the Web. He realised that its 'point and click' approach to navigating the Web was exactly what was needed to transform it from an environment best suited to geeks to a wonderland of information and services for ordinary human beings. He also saw that Mosaic was merely a flawed precursor of the kind of browser that would eventually dominate access to the Internet and decided that he would create a company to design the new generation of Mosaic-derived Internet tools that was needed. His way of doing this was direct and uncompromising. Instead of licensing the Mosaic system from its originators and upgrading it, he poached the people who had created Mosaic in the first place and paid them to start again and design a much better version of the original. The result was Netscape Navigator. Faster and easier to use than Mosaic, Navigator is packed with features including, most significantly, a built-in security system based on a Netscape encryption technology called the secure socket layer (SSL) protocol.

As soon as the first versions of Navigator emerged, Netscape began giving them away as fast as it could. The result has been a dramatic uptake of the software. In January 1995, a survey of 73,000 Web users found that 77 per cent were using one version or another of Netscape's Navigator and even today most agree that Netscape has maintained a share of around 70–80 per cent despite a slew of new browsers coming to market.

Competitors derided the figures saying it was easy to gain market share when you were giving your product away. But they missed the point. Clark was not initially trying to make a business selling browser software. His eye was on a different ball. The importance of getting large numbers of browsers into the market was to create an effective de facto standard. The reason for doing this was to sell not browsers – although Netscape, having established a huge constituency of loyal and committed users, is nowadays starting to charge for updated editions of them – but Web servers. The servers are the computers used to host Web sites and services. The software they run makes them compatible with the Web and proprietary wrinkles allow vendors of servers to offer special Internet features. Most important for Netscape's range is its SSL security system. The important point about such security protocols is that they need two halves of a 'key' to work. One half resides in the server. The other, which enables secure transfers of information, resides in a compatible browser. The heart of Netscape's strategy, therefore, was to inject vast numbers of its browsers into the market and then use the existence of an effective, strong – though not impregnable – security standard based on them to sell its servers. For those looking for a secure basis to begin Internet trading, the servers would look irresistible if virtually everybody on the Internet was already using Netscape's browser.

Domination of server supply means, of course, a lucrative business but, longer term, it also implies a gatekeeping role. The reason is simple. If your browser and server together form the universal standard for Web trading, the commercialisation of the Web stands or falls on your proprietary technology. This means you can manipulate its pricing whenever you wish to control your bottomline performance. You can vary its functionality, so shaping everyone's experience of using the Web. And you can decide who and who not to do business with, so determining who gets access to the commercial opportunities of the Web. In other words, the server–browser equation is strong enough medicine to turn anyone controlling it into the Microsoft of the Internet. And that is exactly what Netscape wants to be.

In practice, of course, it is not as simple as just focusing on security because long term – as we will see later – it will be hard to resist moves to universalise an open, non-proprietary standard. The picture painted above, for example, if it was as crudely drawn in reality, would be given short shrift by US anti-trust legislation. It is not surprising therefore that Netscape has just joined with America Online, Prodigy, CompuServe and IBM to invest in a small software security company called Terisa, which is now charged with creating a single, open security protocol for the Internet. Terisa itself has created the other major Internet security protocol known as Secure HTTP, which is based on a 'public key' cryptography scheme first devised by RSA Data Security. The idea of online and Internet majors investing in it is to merge Netscape's SSL protocol and HTTP into a single, pervasive standard for the future commercialisation of the Internet. Netscape, of course, will try to ensure the final merged product looks much more like SSL than HTTP so that it can leverage its current dominant server–browser position even when the new security standard is established.

Gatekeeping does not have to be based on server–browser strategies. A powerful position can also be built purely on the basis of being a dominant Internet access provider. Although we have already seen what an effective force proprietary networks have become by acting as access providers, major telephone companies also have a powerful position to leverage. The move in 1995 by MCI Communications – the second largest long-distance telephony carrier in the USA – to launch a nationwide dial-up Internet access service called internetMCI, is a good illustration.

Although we had already seen Pacific Bell – the RBOC (Regional Bell Operating Company) serving most telephone users in California – entering the Internet access market with an initiative aimed at business users and we have subsequently seen, in February 1996, AT & T launch its WorldNet service, MCI's move was the first at the time by a US carrier with national reach. As a well-known national organisation with large numbers of existing customers, it was uniquely placed to leverage its existing relationships with subscribers and to build a critical mass of Internet users quickly tied to its proprietary access provision and connection software. At the time, the only other national access providers in the United States – Uunet, Netcom, Holonet and PSI – were relatively small players compared to the financial power and commercial influence of a $13 billion corporation such as MCI.

It is important to assess MCI's move to provide national access to the Internet in the context of another announcement it had made. In addition to its access service, MCI announced it was launching an Internet shopping initiative called marketplaceMCI. This was a secure trading environment based on Netscape server–browser technology within which MCI hoped to gather a powerful group of traders offering an attractive range of purchasable products and services. The key point of MCI's approach was that marketplaceMCI will itself be marketed from MCI's home page – the first site customers are taken to when they log on and – more important, because home pages can be changed by users – it was also to be marketed through all MCI's existing customer links as a telephony provider to millions of businesses and consumers throughout the United States. By building on its existing relationships, MCI could hope to attract large numbers of customers to marketplaceMCI and by making it a compelling environment and by building into it good links with other Web sites, it would have a good chance of making the market-place the definitive jumping off place for Web surfers.

The AT & T initiative, WorldNet, could achieve everything MCI will gain in influence over the Web but on an even bigger scale. AT & T's offering at the time of its launch was extremely attractive to those existing AT & T customers seeking dial-up Internet access. The starting deal for them was five hours of free access per month for a year with additional hours at $2.50. Unlimited access was priced at $19.95 per month. For non-AT & T customers the deal was slightly less attractive with no free access and three hours a month available at a modest $4.95. The totally free service for existing customers was a breakthrough – the first time stand-alone Internet access had been made available at no charge. The aggressive package was all the more powerful because AT & T could immediately leverage a vast, existing customer base of 80 million subscribers. In other words, it was building instant and powerful strategic influence over the Internet in general and the Web in particular by becoming both the portal and facilitator of access for potentially tens of millions of users in the USA and – with WorldNet rolling out worldwide in 1996 – throughout AT & T's international market. With its close individual billing links with every one of those subscribers, a powerhouse like AT & T is perfectly placed to promote particular Internet activities to its constituency and – if it chooses – build an effective Web commerce operation by leveraging its reach.

This is the heart of the new kind of gatekeeping which content – rather than technology – companies can also leverage. As we indicated above, the Web is a complicated and confusing place. It needs beacons to guide people on their journeys. These beacons will define the paths people take and, therefore, whose services they access. A definitive starting point for Web journeys, therefore, will be a powerful arbiter of Web usage. In other words, if MCI or other major access providers can use their success as the springboard for building their home page entry point into the regular first stop for millions of people setting out on the Web, they will have an asset of considerable strategic power and commercial potential. Other organisations, for example, will pay to have links inserted into the key home pages in order to point customers to their sites. There is money to be made and influence to be wielded.

According to a widely publicised statement by MCI's head of Internet initiatives, the Internet pioneer Vint G. Cerf, the combined moves by MCI indicate that it is 'not just a telecommunications company any more'. Since Internet provision is of course a telecommunications service, Cerf's comment indicates that MCI is seeing its future as increasingly linked to content as well as content distribution. In other words, instead of being focused on its role as a carrier, MCI is shaping a strategic future also based on what it carries and – through its influence – making added value out of its ability to shape the pathways that people follow on their journeys around the Web.

The Netscape, MCI and AT & T models add up to the same thing. The biggest game in town, as far as the Internet is concerned, is building influence over how people get access to the Web and what they do while they are using it. There are different ways of playing the game but those who succeed will be the power brokers of what will eventually become the biggest and most influential trading environment the world has ever seen. It is a prize worth fighting for. In fact, in the digital media world, it is probably the only prize worth fighting for.

Home pages – the Web page that a browser starts at when it is launched by a client – are, as the MCI example demonstrates, an important influence on what people do on the Web simply because they can rely on gaining so many eyeballs. The Netscape browser, for example, when purchased from Netscape, opens at the Netscape home page. Although this opening page is only a default setting and can easily be changed by users, the evidence so far suggests that people do not tend to bother. Because Netscape is used by millions, it is not surprising that its home page is one of the busiest places on the Web. It has acquired an instant, ready-made constituency of a size that Web publishers would have to struggle to achieve over months and years of expensive marketing efforts. Having such an instant constituency is only part of the battle. You have to make the initial offering an attractive one or they are likely to overcome their inertia and change the default setting. Netscape has been shrewd – not just in its software strategies but in creating a home site that is dynamic, full of interest and an excellent jumping off place for Web surfers looking for initial directions to take. Netscape offers hot links to other interesting sites and a direct link to key Web directories. Not surprisingly, with a big constituency of users, Netscape is also generating substantial revenues from advertisers who want the millions of eyeballs that Netscape's home page delivers.

The power of the home page has attracted many companies to buy customised versions of standard browsers which default to their home pages so that they can give these away as promotional tools. An entire division of CompuServe is dedicated to developing this kind of business. Already hundreds of companies have taken advantage of the concept. Hotel chains have placed free discs in the rooms of regular guests, for example, while in 1996 Volkswagen of America is giving away Internet software – packaged via a deal with an access provider with some free connect-time – in the glove compartment of every new car it sells and sending similar software out to 500,000 existing customers. It is a scatter gun approach but companies such as Volkswagen are obviously calculating that it makes cost-effective sense to bring traffic – hopefully, long-term traffic – to their home page and via the home page to all the retentive delights of its Web site.

The same theme of leveraging influence over how people use the Web lies at the heart of all Web publishing strategies. Most of all, of course, the central objective is to influence people to visit sites – and keep visiting them. By implication, this asks the question: what are companies really trying to achieve by building and operating Web sites? There is no single answer because objectives vary with types of companies. In some cases, there is no answer because there is no objective. In other words, some companies build their sites without even thinking through their reasons for doing so. Content companies, however, have a clear objective: they plan to commercialise some form of content asset, either leveraged out of assets they already possess in the 'real' world or via assets newly created for the online environment. The majority are seeking, more or less directly, to extend the potential of existing content and its branding. For these companies the process of Web publishing has three key phases. First, use existing brand power to build an online franchise. Second, use the franchise to create a constituency – an audience that will be loyally tied to regular use of the site. Third, commercialise the constituency. This is not rocket science – the magazine and newspaper industries have been doing it for years. What is new now, however, is the peculiar and distinctive characteristics of online environments and, most of all, how people use them.

Before we examine these issues in more detail, it is worth pausing to re-examine a word we have been using repeatedly and without qualification, as if its meaning and significance were self-evident. The word is 'content' and in the online world it needs some careful re-evaluation.

CONTENT AND ONLINE SUCCESS

The overheated and overhyped world of the Web is putting increasing pressure on content organisations of all kinds. The issue is no longer whether to create a Web presence but to decide urgently the when, how and what of that presence. Naturally enough, many companies are snatching online strategies out of the air, deciding abruptly either to get onto the Web or do a deal with Microsoft or one of the other proprietary majors or both. Sometimes fast, tactical moves work but there is already evidence that many companies – particularly those new to network publishing – are not taking the time they need to think through the realities of the new market-place, to determine where real strategic advantage lies, what existing assets they can deploy, which new ones they will have to acquire to ensure success and, at the end of the day, what kind of business model will make serious money for them long term.

The only good online strategies begin with some simple questions. What are we trying to achieve by going online? What are our expectations? What resources and assets can we deploy? What level of commitment can we afford? Where are we weak and where are we strong? Any MBA (Master of Business Administration) graduate worth his or her salt would consider these commonplace basics but the feverish atmosphere surrounding the apparent rapid emergence of a consumer online market is in danger of sweeping away common-sense deliberations of this kind. Content companies, in particular, need to draw a deep breath before taking action. A time for cool contemplation is vital. But the pressure is growing on them to move quickly and that largely manufactured sense of urgency is pushing them to take precipitate action. It is true of course that some urgency does exist – particularly where the Web is concerned. The recent frantic pioneering activity is based on a sound policy – staking out franchises early, even before the Web can be commercialised in order to be well positioned when it is. But rushing to establish those franchises and getting it wrong could be as disastrous as thinking that the Web in particular and online in general fails the so-what test.

The worst danger for content companies is that they actually believe that – in a traditional sense – content is still really king. It is the most dangerous kind of false reassurance because it contains an element of truth. But the broader reality is that it is much more than content as we have always known it that determines online success. The real threat is that the idea of content always being the dictator of commercial advantage makes owners of content complacent and less likely to take the right action at the right time.

To illustrate this we can take a brief look at some of the major issues involved in creating an effective Web presence. There are a raft of practical and technical issues, of course, which shape the design of the site, its capabilities and – most important – the costs associated with creating and running it long term. It is clear, for example, that we must increasingly try to design our sites today with the Web technologies of tomorrow. During 1996 and 1997 the experience of using the Web will have changed beyond recognition. It will commonly offer such features as real-time audio from sites, voice communications, three-dimensional graphics and virtual reality-like experiences and – within limitations – the delivery of short, windowed video clips in more or less real time. What we can offer from these sites a year hence both in terms of an online sensation as well as basic commercial products and services will be dramatically different from the possibilities being exploited today. So we have to embrace the future in today's design and build everything we do with an easy and immediate upgrade path. In this crucial sense, the Web is and will remain a highly dynamic environment.

But to put traditional content in perspective, we need to concentrate on more general issues of site design. Here too it is vital to understand the Web as a dynamic place but in a different sense. One of the most powerful attributes of online publishing is its ability to deliver fast-changing information. In the professional and corporate market, the power of online systems to deliver volatile information, even information updated on a moment by moment basis, has been one of the key foundations of what is today a $13 billion business. Users of online systems expect and demand dynamic information. They do not want to read the same information or undergo the same experience every time they visit an online site. Going online is ultimately a communications experience and, like a conversation, what you expect to get out of it is something constantly changing. Saying or hearing the same thing over and again is simply too boring to be tolerated. In other words, Web design must embody a strategy for constantly varying, updating, upgrading the content of the site.

Communications itself is a key notion too. If using the Web is essentially a communications experience, it is largely because that is what people want it to be. While it is already evident that users of online services have a relatively few favourite things they like doing online (spending money, as we have noted, is not one of them!) the one thing that is consistently high on their priorities is sharing and exchanging information and ideas with other people. And if that is what people most like doing online, it clearly must – interpreted sensitively – be a thread of all good Web design.

So Web sites must be dynamic and communications based. But there is a third crucial ingredient. The experience of using online services is very personal. If communing with an online site is more like making a telephone call than reading a book, then users of the Web want sites to respond to them personally. This means Web design is about marketing to one person and seeing a constituency of users as a collection of well-defined and well-understood individuals. Personalising Web sites is not easy but with the right software tools and server systems it is increasingly possible to achieve. At the simplest level, customisation of this kind means that visitors to a site are welcomed with a personal message and a range of suggestions of what they may like to access based on their previous visits and the interests they showed during them. At more sophisticated levels, sites will increasingly offer fully filtered and bespoke information services.

None of this has much to do with our traditional notion of static, analogue content. And the implication is that owners of content may not be able to deploy as much of their existing content assets on the Web as they might suppose. Indeed, many are already concluding that the very idea of content on the Web – or any other network publishing environment – needs to be redefined. Building an online strategy, therefore, may well start with biting a very painful bullet indeed. We may have to accept that traditional content – important as it may be – is far from king on the Web. What really counts is understanding customers and building individual relationships with them. This is what lies at the heart of online success.

COMMERCIALISING A WEB SITE

If a site is successful in staking out its franchise and creating a constituency of long-term users of the site, how can it turn its promising position into one that generates substantial revenues? One thing is sure, it will need to do this quickly because the cost of entry for those aiming to build substantial and effective Web publishing operations is no longer modest. There was once a view that the attraction of the Web was the cheapness of being there. A few thousand dollars could buy the hardware, software and connection to get a server linked to the Internet. This is still true: it does cost only a few thousand dollars – so long as you do not plan to do anything significant with the Web presence that you have created. A powerful site capable of building a substantial constituency – and retaining it – needs major upfront investment and, just as important, substantial ongoing investment to keep the site fresh, dynamic and on the leading edge of Web technology and functionality. The best commercial sites currently operating have dollar budgets well into eight figures per annum and – like making a movie, computer game or multimedia CD-ROM title – there is effectively no limit to what can be spent. So, with the cost on entry soaring, the pressure on revenue generation is increasingly intense.

The first understanding that site owners must have – whatever media culture they come from – is that to stand any chance of profitability, sites will almost certainly need multiple sources of revenue. This is a familiar idea, for example, to magazine companies but a strange and largely alien one, say, for book publishers. However, it is crucial, particularly in these early pioneering years, because no one yet fully understands where the main emphasis in revenue generation will ultimately come from. Until this becomes clearer, everyone trying to make money from costly Web presences must look for revenue from every possible source. That is why today's operators of Web shopping malls are likely to fail – because they have committed their business model to attracting visitors to their sites and then commercialising those visits via a single form of revenue generation. Of course, business models are never blunt instruments and there will, in practice, be many variations but multiplicity is a vital key in searching for ways of making the Web viable. There are at least four major paradigms for revenue generation – others, no doubt, will emerge:

- Selling content
- Selling advertising
- Conducting transactions
- Selling links

SELLING CONTENT

First, sites can create revenue from attempting to sell content or, more likely, access to content. The distinction is a fine and important one. There is a deep-rooted fear among traditional content companies that once they post their copyright assets on the Web, they will quickly be plundered. Like much of the concern surrounding security on the Web, this particular fear is based more on a perception than a reality. It also represents a danger for such traditional players who have always created businesses out of a balance between both protecting and simultaneously exploiting copyrights. At any time it is a difficult balancing act. But in the Web environment, there is a strong sense that protection is almost impossible and exploitation, at best, problematic. This analysis would, catastrophically, counsel content companies to steer clear of the Web altogether. Fortunately, it is becoming clear, even to newcomers to the field, that protection is possible – at least to levels comparable to the real world – and that the best possible protection is not to make copyright materials accessible online in the first place. Instead, they can be showcased on the Web and sold via conventional channels. Showcasing itself can be a sophisticated process, including a sampling of the content products. Much here depends on the type of content involved. For television, video and film companies, showcasing and promotion is really the only option. Supplying product is still far beyond the capabilities of the Web. New forms of compression technologies, however, are beginning to make 'good enough' real-time video on a small window of the PC screen – probably adequate for sampling products – a near-term possibility.

For record companies, showcasing and sampling is already a possibility using existing, widely available software, although quality is still relatively poor, certainly inferior to normal CD quality sound. In other words, like the video companies, music companies (and the bands and artists themselves) are unlikely – with exceptions such as operations like the Internet Underground Music Archive in the United States and Cerberus in the UK – to attempt to deliver their products over the networks. Print publishers, of course, are the media players with most to lose and gain right now from posting their content directly on the Web because the environment is most immediately suited to text leavened with a few illustrations. There are, of course, resolution and convenience issues – resolution determined both by the way the content is stored in the server and by the limitations of the output printer and convenience by the fact that large volumes even of mere text can take time to download over ordinary dial-up connections. For publishers, therefore, the issue is most immediate but, even for them, the obvious solution is to consider promoting rather than selling their crown jewels. That way they can be stolen only in the real world, not in cyberspace. In any event, as we saw in the previous section, the notion of content of the Web needs careful definition. While the Web may become a place where some traditional content is traded, it is more a place where trade will be based on very different notions of content than previously understood by the media industry. In fact, the old forms do not sit well in the new world. The type of content that flourishes on the Web is much more an experience than a fixed body of intellectual property in the traditional sense. This makes it much harder for Web content to be stolen. After all, how do you steal an experience? Only with great difficulty.

Even more difficult, right now, is actually generating revenue by selling access to content – whether defined in traditional or new era terms. Content, of course, drives the success of a site – by definition since there is no site without content – but to get customers to part with money for access to it is a real challenge. Those who have attempted to charge have seen the size of their constituencies plunge. On the face of it, this seems a strange difficulty. After all, most of the media industry is – on the surface, at least – based on the idea of selling access to content to those who want or need it. The direct exploitation of the content is the principal source of revenue generation. On the Web, by contrast, content is the honey that attracts interest and helps build a constituency. Revenue generation seems to come later. In fact, closer analysis shows us that even in real world media sectors, revenue generation is often more complex. Successful films produce substantial box office revenues but can often make more from video and merchandising exploitations. Magazines and newspapers rely on their content to sustain communities of regular readers which, in turn, are attractive to advertisers. Even book publishers – most obviously associated with single revenue stream businesses – actually make substantial sums from selling to third parties what they term 'subsidiary rights': the rights to serialise, adapt, anthologise original printed works or to turn books into different copyright forms such as films, plays, television programmes or even interactive products. So, in reality, the media world is less attached to just selling its content directly and is more multistream than one might suppose.

Strategies for generating revenue from access to content resolve themselves into four options. Selling access to an entire site by charging a subscription for entry is the most obvious approach. It also appears doomed to failure at present except for sites offering professional and corporate information with a strong 'need to know' character. The majority of consumer sites would find it very difficult to persuade customers to pay in such a blunt fashion. Only slightly less blunt is the idea of charging for access to content on a 'pay as you go' basis. Instead of a fixed entry fee, customers buy such content as they choose à la carte. More subtle and therefore more plausible is the widely favoured approach of providing site access free and creating a high value, premium area within the site. Those wanting to get into the premium area have to buy a password which gives them access for a subscription period. Examples of early experiments with this approach include Penthouse, Hachette Fillipachi's 'Car and driver' site and the hugely successful Sportszone, run by US sports TV giant, ESPN. More subtle still – but possibly less plausible – is the move to blur the distinction between charging for content and charging for Internet access. A number of service providers – particularly news publishers – are now offering a subscription which includes an Internet access deal. The package is created by the content company sub-contracting the access provision to a third party company whose main business is providing such access. The content company hopes to negotiate preferential rates for its subscribers so the overall deal looks attractive. But the reality, of course, is that the charge for content and access combined always adds up to more than access alone and customers only have to do some simple mental arithmetic to appreciate the level of charging being made for the content to which they gain access. So the technique has some psychological value in fudging content charges but is not likely to fool many of the people for much of the time. That said, the deal could still look attractive if access was being provided at a heavily discounted rate. But to get a really good deal on access, the content company would have to guarantee some fairly high volume of trade.

The difficulty of selling content online is striking. In the real world there appears to be little difficulty so long as the content offering is compelling and the price is right. There is probably a slew of complex reasons but one is clear. In our current media culture, people value atoms more readily than they value bits. In other words, if a digital product is enshrined in a physical medium, immediately palpable to the senses, it is more easily regarded as an object of inherent value. By contrast, if a product is delivered online as a stream of bits, those accessing it seem less willing to appreciate its lasting value and are accordingly less inclined to pay for it. This phenomenon – which may decline as the generations roll by – is not helped by current Internet culture where information is widely seen – almost in terms of an ideology – as something that should be freely available. Even with the old altruistic culture fast being swept away by today's hardnosed commercial initiatives, the instinct that information delivered via the bitstream should be free lingers on and makes those initiatives that much harder to consummate.

SELLING ADVERTISING

Perhaps as obvious as the idea of selling content is the prospect of selling advertising. Currently the most widely emphasised approach to revenue generation, the sale of advertising on a Web site is based fundamentally on that site's guaranteed ability to deliver eyeballs to the merchants taking the advertising space. In other words, a site's ability to attract advertisers and maintain a highly priced rate card is directly proportional to the size and focus of the constituency of users. Both factors – size and focus – are crucial. A large but demographically unfocused constituency may be desirable but a smaller but more focused one might be more so. In other words, size is not everything. If a site becomes the definitive stopping-off place for the world's fly fishermen, for example, the raw size of the constituency is less important than the fact that potential advertisers have a clear idea of main interests of the individuals making it up. Plainly such a site represents a golden opportunity for certain kinds of advertisers while others can avoid wasting their money.

Clearly, this argument holds good for both Web sites and proprietary online services. Most proprietary majors, however, have large unfocused constituencies with the important proviso that large means very large indeed. At the time of writing, for example, CompuServe has about 3.5 million subscribers worldwide while AOL counts over 4 million. These are big constituencies even if they represent a very mixed bag of individuals. On sheer size alone, they are potentially attractive to advertisers. However, proprietaries by their nature offer a wide variety of offerings to their subscribers and advertisers can therefore get the opportunity to lodge adverts in areas of the service which attract demographically focused subsets of the overall constituency and so meet their need to spend their money addressing not just eyeballs but the right eyeballs.

Estimates vary wildly about how much advertising is currently taking place online. The US analysts Forrester Research believe that only about $10 million was spent in 1995 but that the scale of advertising will rapidly escalate over the next few years reaching a total spend of $2.2 billion by the year 2000. The reality of 1995 was probably closer to a spend of $60 million but whatever the exact figure, most analysts agree that the number is small. The steep escalation in revenue is based on three major factors coming into play over the years leading to the millennium. First, the emergence of effective ways to audit the effect of advertising on the Web. Software solutions are already emerging to address this issue. Second, a growing confidence and understanding by advertisers of how to utilise the interactive medium and leverage, in particular, its potential one-to-oneness. And third, the rise of standardised and trusted mechanisms to allow secure payments to be made over Internet connections.

Whatever the future may hold, it seems clear that substantial advertising revenues are being generated by only a relatively few high profile sites. In the course of 1995, for example, the HotWired site announced it was cash positive on the basis of its steadily growing income from advertising. Other sites such as Web directories and search engines – Yahoo, Lycos and others – key home pages, such as Netscape's, and highly popular content offerings, such as Sportszone, are all generating serious income. Elsewhere, advertising and advertising rate cards are more patchy. One thing is clear, however.

All site owners with a consumer emphasis are chasing advertising as the key revenue source for their Web operations.

As we noted above, advertisers are undoubtedly at a disadvantage right now and the position will change only slowly. The key gap in the Web offering, as far as they are concerned, is auditing mechanisms for Web sites. Not only are advertisers seeking the right constituencies to address, they want to know which individuals in those constituencies have accessed their adverts and with what effect. In other words, advertisers seek some plausible way of measuring Web activity to tell them whether they are spending their (or their client's) advertising dollars effectively. Proprietary networks can deliver this because users accessing their services are individually identifiable and their actions online can be tracked step by step of the way. By contrast, the position for Web sites is more difficult. The technology of the Web makes it hard for site proprietors or advertisers to identify visitors unless they are required to register themselves beforehand. This is accordingly a widely used technique. Registration processes and passwords, even when no charge is being made for site access, however, are time consuming and tedious and are hardly an encouragement to new users or old ones who have (inevitably) forgotten their password. Even if sites can identify visitors, tracking what they do while connected to the site is a complex process and software – such as I/Pro or NetCount – is only now emerging capable of delivering useful data beyond the usual counting of so-called 'hits' which is no more than adding up the number of hypertext links on pages accessed by users while visiting a site. Other software designed to analyse increasingly more sophisticated usage data is also becoming available and packages such as Interse's Market Focus and Open Market's WebReporter are becoming popular to save the laborious efforts of manual analysis.

There is still much progress to be made in this area of site exploitation and imminent developments will make a vast difference to the viability of sites, particularly because of the appeal that fully analysed tracking data have for advertisers. However, while server side usage and auditing software has a crucial role to play, client software is also going to contribute enormously to the personalising of site responses to incoming browsers. Netscape's browser for example now embodies a software system known as 'persistent client state HTTP cookies'. The cookies exist in the browser in order to allow site owners to tie together the various requests that a browser makes during a visit to the site. So, instead of seeing client activity as a flow of seemingly unrelated hits, site owners can see a client visit as a contiguous session and thereby analyse usage data far more powerfully. Cookies in Netscape browsers are identifiers which maintain and store information about a visitor's use of the site during the course of a single visit. The same cookies can contain information about the kind of browser, where it has been before it visited the site and, potentially, demographic data about the browser's user. In other words, if the cookie concept is more fully developed, it could effectively add to browsers a personalised identity card enabling sites to respond in a much more targeted way to visitors than they can at present.

An example of how this principle is already being used comes from the San Francisco based online specialist, C/Net. Using its own bespoke software, C/Net offers the opportunity to advertisers to tune their propositions differently for different site visitors. By using a mix of analysis of the incoming browser header information – which indicates the domain name and software identity of incoming browsers – and of registration data stored at the server based on personal information volunteered by visitors, C/Net can automatically provide basic demographic data to advertisers who can then deliver messages with emphases appropriate to the individuals accessing their advertising. For example, a computer supplier can ensure that the advert a Mac user sees does not try to sell PC products. Another advertiser might emphasise a corporate role in school resources for incoming browsers with 'edu' domain names and vary the offering to stress strengths in working with public sector organisations if the domain is 'gov'. Registration data could help a car manufacturer target older visitors with messages stressing safety and reliability while younger visitors receive a variant which focuses on a car's performance and design qualities. This approach to individualising site response is still in its infancy but is a crucially important future direction. Leveraging its potential, intense one-to-oneness lies at the heart of the successful commercialisation of the Web and the future of the entire online industry hangs upon it.

While the path of future direction is clear, the present reality is that for most Web sites, counting hits is the best that can be offered. Understandably, therefore, advertisers are currently cautious or undecided about the pace of their move online. The potential benefits seem clear – access to global audiences or demographically defined cuts thereof and the possibility of forging powerful, one-to-one relationships with individuals – but the price being asked plays badly against the current lack of measurable feedback. Advertisers simply do not have the reassurance they need yet that each dollar they spend online is best spent online. But advertisers face an even more challenging issue which many are only slowly beginning to appreciate. The nature of advertising online is fundamentally different from the processes of advertising in the traditional media world. The techniques that work on television or in print do not necessarily transfer to online environments and advertisers – together with all the content players of the old media industry – have to be prepared to re-engineer their skills and commercial understandings in order to make their businesses work. Most importantly, interactive advertising is a one-to-one experience so far as the audience is concerned. Accessing an advert is a deliberate act by an individual and if the person has been persuaded to access it, the advert needs to deliver some real benefit. Punchy appeals for attention, or loud single-idea strap lines to sell a brand message, do not work online.

To be effective, advertising has to adapt to the new medium and that means close targeting of the audience, the use of communications to create two-way relationships with the audience and an increasing and deliberate blurring of the distinction between advertising and content. Such a blurring causes immediate concerns among regulators who are rightly dedicated to ensuring people know what is an advert and what is objective content without an advertising axe to grind. But it is possible to see the process as a benign means of supporting central content offerings with advertising content – information that is contextualised with the content to which it is related and which adds value to it. Additionally, the advertising must be genuinely interactive. It is not good enough to re-purpose advertising from the real world. Online must have what online needs and what online needs is the same for content sites as it is for advertising. So, whether a content site hosts an advertiser's offering or points from a button on the site to the advertiser's own site, it is vital that the content owner does more than sell space and walk away from the transaction. It is essential for site owners to develop a close, creative understanding with its advertisers so that the two communities can work together to create advertising that supports content and content that supports advertising. A meeting of minds is needed and every effort should be expended to achieve it. Interactive advertising in general and online advertising in particular will never work without it.

Conducting transactions

A third key revenue stream is based on offering Web constituencies the opportunity to conduct transactions online. This has been the great hope of the consumer online networks for over a decade. It is no accident that Prodigy, for example, is partly owned by US retailing giant Sears. The original concept was that having won a large base of subscribers, Prodigy could turn into a huge, home shopping environment in which billions of dollars of business would be transacted by merchants, each of whom would pay Prodigy a small slice of the action. In fact, by 1993, electronic shopping barely accounted for 2 per cent of Prodigy's revenues. The other proprietaries have had similar success.

The mood is changing, however, and the belief is growing that as serious volumes of users emerge, home shopping will come into its inheritance as one of the major revenue generators of the online industry. With the Web expanding rapidly, opportunities for this kind of trade appear to be exploding. Analysts and forecasters are falling over themselves to predict the sheer size of the emerging market-place. Depending on who you listen to, the market could be worth anything from $6 billion to $300 billion by the turn of the century – a sure indication that no one really knows. The sense so far among home shopping specialists is that if the virtual shops and malls are built, the customers will come. Even if they do come, of course, it is worth remembering for the sake of perspective that even the most optimistic estimates of the market look tiny compared to real world shopping. The retail grocery market in the United States alone is currently worth half a trillion dollars per annum.

The reality of home shopping on proprietary services has been that the opportunities to shop have been limited to relatively few suppliers who have offered a largely unappealing shopping experience. Indeed, it is questionable whether any true shopping experience can be delivered online – replete with its essential elements of entertainment, serendipity and socialising. Probably the best that can be offered is a reliable buying experience majoring on the fact that online shops can offer limitless shelf space with a comprehensive range of products. They are also best at selling commodities rather than products with varied values and benefits. Because of this, online is a good place to offer access to large catalogues of media and software products which can be ordered online and fulfilled by conventional channels. It is not surprising, therefore, that in surveys of those online shoppers that could be found in the United States in 1995, 48 per cent tended to buy computer software and 34 per cent purchased entertainment products, especially music CDs and, to a much lesser extent, books and videos. Most (about 74 per cent) cited convenience as the main reason for shopping online. Strikingly, only a minority favoured specially created shopping mall sites to make purchases with nearly 70 per cent tending to conduct transactions at single sites which provided a transactional facility as a strand of their offering.

This suggests a powerful idea about shopping online. The fact that services on single sites are most popular may suggest that online shopping works best when the transaction facility is placed close to the point of interest that drives the impulse to buy. To understand this idea better, consider a simple example. One of the earliest pioneers of Web sites among the record companies was US label Geffen. Today at the Geffen site you can surf through a range of attractive pages that tell you more than most would want to know about Geffen artists and recordings, all colourfully illustrated and complete with sound samples. Strategically placed among the pages are buttons with the words 'I want this CD now!' written on them. Not surprisingly, the buttons occur next to some of the most persuasive descriptions of latest album releases. By clicking the button, the user is instantly hyperlinked to another site run by a direct mail CD specialist called CD Now which has created a massive CD shopping presence on the Web. The link does not simply take the user to the front door of CD Now's shop, it takes them directly to that location within CD Now where users can place an order for the album they have just been reading about.

In other words, the impulse to buy has been commercialised by Geffen (and, incidentally, by CD Now) at the very moment the impulse is generated.

This is a powerful model for the future of online shopping because it places shopping, like advertising, in close proximity to content. Indeed, just as we argued for advertising, online shopping may be best expressed as a strand within content, contextualised and supporting the content experience.

Currently, online shopping remains in its infancy and faces particular problems on the Web. Most obvious is the issue of security on the Web and the lack of effective electronic payment mechanisms that will allow customers both to place an order and pay for the goods in a single, safe and reliable transaction. Proprietary networks have never had this problem because all data moving through their networks pass exclusively through their own infrastructures and, thanks to established subscriber management systems, consolidating online purchases within normal billing mechanisms is a simple process. On the Web, by contrast, concern about secure payment is probably the single most important factor inhibiting the growth of Web commerce. We will consider security and payment mechanisms briefly later but for now we need only note that – despite the depth of concern that is evident among Web users – trustworthy technical solutions are rapidly emerging which will provide a small number of dominant standards by sometime in 1997 which will spark rapid and sustained growth in Web commerce during 1998 and beyond.

As a revenue-generating option, however, transactions look like a strong possibility for the medium-term future. The potential, as with advertising, is based upon the creation by distinctive and successful sites of established constituencies. Just as advertisers will pay for access to such constituencies, so will merchants with offerings appropriate to the demographic of the constituency.

SELLING LINKS

Once a site has established its franchise and built a constituency it is able to influence that constituency in important ways. Most important for proprietors of related but non-competing sites, is the possibility of gaining traffic from the 'hot' site by persuading the site owner to point its constituency at them. So far, this kind of hotlinking is usually agreed on a largely reciprocal basis but once sites have established themselves as successful and well used, they can drive much harder bargains. To some extent, the desire to generate revenue from hotlinking must be balanced with the need to add value to one site by providing links to others of related interest. Such linking is a key feature in determining a site's attractiveness and it would be ill judged to sacrifice good linking possibilities simply because a site is unable to generate revenue from the link destinations.

More interesting than one successful site merely generating hard cash by trading its constituency by selling links is the possibility of agreeing deals with paid-for sites to get preferential access terms for constituents. Proprietors of premium sites or premium areas within sites will be inclined to give substantial discounts in return for a guaranteed flow of traffic. Meantime, site owners can offer an even more attractive package for access to their own sites by, perhaps, making a subscription charge that includes free access to a number of otherwise paid-for sites. In other words, this kind of deal allows major Web sites to become packagers of other sites, offering a low-cost point of entry to a range of content and service experiences which, paid for individually, would amount to a substantial monthly cost. The key building block, however, is the ownership of a constituency which, either through raw size or valuable demographic focus, can be readily traded with others.

THE IMPACT ON PROPRIETARY NETWORKS

The idea of Web sites turning themselves into packagers of other sites may sound familiar. In fact, this emerging model for Web trade is a direct analogue of the traditional offering to subscribers of proprietary online networks. As we saw in chapter 5, the essential proposition of such services was to offer a low cost key which would confer access to a warehouse of other people's content, licensed in by the proprietary services. Even though in practice little revenue has been generated for the third party content owners, the proposition for them was clear and apparently attractive. While network customers would have access to their content, they would have access to the customers. And networks boasting millions of subscribers had a very compelling carrot to offer to content companies with little other option for gaining access to online exploitation.

Ironically, the original proposition for both customers and content providers was viable only so long as there was no consumer online market. As soon as the market emerged, the basic model began to crack under the strain of competitive pressure. The major proprietary services were desperate for market share – particularly since increasing the number of their subscribers was the only way they could boost their revenues. As we saw in chapter 5, online subscribers are reluctant to spend money online and the revenues generated from subscriber bases was therefore largely governed by the price of the subscription and how many subscriptions a network operator could sell. The battle for subscribers sent subscriptions and connect-time charges tumbling and as they tumbled – and subscriber numbers rose – the potential returns for content providers, who were usually paid on a percentage of connect-time charges or a slice of subscription revenues for new customers they brought to the network, began to tumble with them.

At the same time, a new and urgent element in the battle among proprietaries to win market share was the need to distinguish their offerings, particularly by including in their warehouses some highly branded crown jewel content which none of their competitors could offer. For a few content owners, therefore, Christmas had come early because, while the majority of content companies were getting next to nothing, a few were being wooed by proprietaries offering high guaranteed payments just to get hold of exclusive access to a leading brand. In an important sense, therefore, the boot was very much on the other foot. Proprietaries had originally driven a hard deal with content owners, taking everything in terms of brand value and consumer usage data and offering them little in return. This, in a curious way, was sustainable so long as there was only a small market for online services. Once the market emerged – at a gallop – content was a key factor in the battle to win customers away from competitors and content was, therefore, in a far stronger negotiating position. This is the reason why in the two years before 1994 and 1996 the original 80:20 deal in favour of the networks flipped into a 20:80 deal favouring content.

A further nail in the coffin of the traditional proprietary business model was the emergence of the Web. One very powerful reason why proprietaries were always strongly placed in negotiating with content was that content had nowhere else to go in order to gain online exploitation. The proprietaries had invested hundreds of millions of dollars building a communications and computing infrastructure that would enable them to reach the market. The huge cost of entry, therefore, meant that content owners simply had to do business with the established network because the prospect of them building their own networks was unthinkable. The emergence of the Web changed all that and it did so quickly and decisively. For the first time, content had an alternative to doing business with the proprietaries. It could invest just a few tens of thousands of dollars and instantly gain independent online access to a global market-place numbered in millions. On the face of it, the ease, autonomy and reach of the Web looks almost irresistible.

For the proprietaries, this new development made an increasingly difficult situation desperate. Not only did they now have to compete with one another for content, but also they had to compete with the lure of the Web. Their response has turned out to be a powerful one, although it implies a complete revision of their original business models. The first step in the response was to recognise that millions of consumers were seeking safe, reliable and cheap access to the Internet. Most were getting such access via independent Internet service providers (ISPs) who were buying bandwidth from telephone companies in order to gain a pipe into the backbones of the Internet. Many were small start-up, serving relatively small areas, while a few were better funded, larger entities with national and international ambitions. For the proprietary networks, the idea of also offering Internet access was a natural and inevitable step. Whether they saw the Internet as their potential nemesis or not, they had to recognise that many of their existing subscribers were interested in the Internet and that potential subscribers would be even more attracted to a proprietary if Internet access was just another part of its overall offerings. The proprietaries would probably have preferred to de-invent the Internet. But since that was hardly an option, they reckoned that people would get Internet access if they wanted it and that they might as well get it from them. Whatever their reservations about the Internet, therefore, the proprietaries determined to make Internet access another of their offerings.

This first step – forced upon them by the realities of the market-place – has quickly led to a much fuller acceptance of the Internet. Within months of beginning to offer access during the early part of 1994, the proprietaries realised that they could deploy a much deeper business strategy. It became clear that offering Internet access was quickly turning into a major attraction for both existing and new subscribers with literally hundreds of thousands of customers signing up for it within months of the access deal becoming available.

Prodigy – otherwise the laggard of the three proprietary majors – beat its competitors to the starting post, largely because it had already decided in 1993 to completely revise its very poor user interface and to create a new one based on HTML code, the underlying language of the Web. In January 1995, Prodigy launched its first Web browser, making it available to its existing customers by downloading, and also began offering Internet access through its network. By March, 450,000 people had downloaded the software, of whom half were new customers who signed up after the Web access was announced. In under two months, Prodigy had become a bigger Web access provider than Netcom, formerly the largest ISP in the United States. CompuServe launched its Web service next and AOL followed about mid-year. All found their offerings highly popular and saw growth in subscriber numbers – already strong – accelerate dramatically. Proprietaries quickly saw that being the point of access for such huge numbers of Internet users gave them – like MCI, AT & T and other big national and international players – a powerful influence over what people did when they used the Internet.

In particular, they could influence the use of the Web and the sites their customers were most likely to visit. Prodigy's early experience confirmed what is now confirmed by subsequent more general research on Web usage: the majority of Web users pay regular visits to only a handful of sites. This immediately suggested to the proprietaries that they could add immediate value to their access provision by including, within their own proprietary infrastructure, copies of the most popular sites. The advantages of doing this are substantial. For example, many popular Web sites can accommodate only a few hundred – or at best a very few thousand – simultaneous visitors before the server locks out any others trying to gain access. A typical site cached within a proprietary network and leveraging the powerful proprietary infrastructure can handle tens of thousands of visitors at one time. Beyond the ability to handle large numbers of visitors, caching also makes accessing sites faster and more consistent. In other words, even users with slow modems will get an acceptable experience of accessing cached sites and the speed of access will not vary with the changing overall traffic on the Internet, a frustrating phenomenon which makes general Web access fast one moment and painfully slow the next. The resulting proposition to customers was a strong one for the proprietaries and an important extension of their original positioning. In spring 1995, Ted Leonis, president of America Online services, used a striking and unusual metaphor to encapsulate the new offering. He likened the new proprietary model based on the cruise line business with the cruises being voyages of discovery on the Web.

'I see us becoming the Carnival Cruise Lines of this business,' he said.

> Carnival [gives you] predictable pricing. Your fare, your activities on the boat, all your meals are included. No surprises. Your berth is going to be clean, and it's going to be safe . . . . When you pull into a port, Carnival plans your day for you. They say: ' . . . for those of you who like scuba diving, here are the best places to go and here are the authorized guides. For those of you who want to go shopping, we'll take you into town. If you're looking for jewelry, we feel comfortable with these two or three chains. In fact, if you present them your berth card, you'll get a ten per cent discount.'

The last point is a telling one and it relates directly to our remarks about generating strategic advantage from pointing constituencies at paid-for sites. With massive constituencies, the proprietaries can now offer chosen Web sites the prospect of huge volumes of traffic. This can be done by pointing (and otherwise promoting) from within the proprietary infrastructure to sites outside it or by mirroring external sites and making them effectively a part of the infrastructure. Either way, the proprietaries can negotiate good deals for their customers, either getting discounts or free access (with the site's reduced charge carried by the proprietary).

As this new business emerged – with proprietaries for the first time embracing content that was not proprietary to them – other signs of the shift towards a Web-centric future emerged. While retaining the idea of a proprietary environment as a part (rather than the entirety) of their offerings, proprietaries also decided to hitch their wagons to the increasing number of major content companies setting up their independent online presence on the Web. They did this by mingling two strands. One was offering services that actually helped content find its way onto the Web. These services included consultancy and the opportunity to use the proprietaries' powerful access infrastructure to speed access to sites. The other strand was to joint venture the development of such sites with content partners and so, for the first time, take a direct equity stake in content assets. In both cases, the thrust of the development was to build new and closer links with content because the proprietaries perceived deep relationships with content to be the means by which they could simultaneously leverage the power of content to generate traffic and revenue on the Web and their ability to powerfully promote selected content offerings.

At a technical level, proprietaries began to shift their user interfaces Webwards too with browsers emerging as de facto standards. Indeed, newcomers to the proprietary business – especially in European outfits like UK Online and Europe Online – were effectively creating themselves as large, complex sites on the Web with content on their sites and a multitude of links to chosen external sites. Users could come and go from the strictly proprietary area – the large Web site forming the hub of their offering – and explore the further reaches of the Web or, at their choice, stick to the online environment defined by the proprietary's strategic links. The Microsoft proprietary initiative has been reinvented by Microsoft to reflect this concept with MSN effectively becoming an influential point of access to the web and its proprietary offerings being, effectively, heavily promoted Web sites with preferential access available to its own MSN constituency.

This hints at the long-term future of the proprietary business, no longer as distinct from the Web but as super-sites on the Web. In other words, the Internet and the Web become the defining factor with which all online service providers align themselves. This is the heart of the revolution which the Internet has begun.

SECURITY AND WEB PAYMENTS

The commercialising of the Web depends fundamentally on being able to send messages to and from servers and clients in complete security. Much else may depend on this but being able to complete financial transactions is totally governed by it. Beyond security lies the issue of how such transactions are consummated in terms of mechanisms to handle the payments themselves, particularly when those payments may come from hundreds of thousands, even millions, of geographically dispersed individuals and the size of each of the transactions can, ideally, vary from a few cents to very large sums. The emerging systems aimed at providing such secure payment mechanisms are highly technical and commercially complex. In this section, therefore, we will not attempt to be exhaustive in our treatment but will aim to establish basic concepts and to paint the main strategic headlines. For those seeking more detail, there is plenty of material freely available on the Web itself.

Why is Internet security such a concern? The reason has to do with the way in which the Internet is organised to convey information between users. If you are a CompuServe user and you send a message via Compu-Serve to another user, the bits representing your message flow only through CompuServe's own computer infrastructure. If an Internet user sends a message, it may pass through hundreds of other people's computers on its way to its destination as it is switched from backbone to backbone across the globe. The fear that haunts the Internet community is that cyber fraudsters are lurking out on the networks hanging around switching points with sniffer programs that can invade other people's data and either copy or alter them. In particular, there are programs which can spot packets of data containing the configuration of digits that suggest the data are carrying a credit card number. The reality behind this fear is far less alarming. Apart from a few well-publicised cases of such fraud, there is no serious evidence that posting your credit card number on the Internet is any more perilous than giving your card to a waiter in a restaurant. The intensity of the concern therefore is based on a perception among users that the mysterious and abstract network with all its metaphorically open doors is a dangerous place for sensitive information. Security systems, therefore, work not only in the territory of technology but also in the realm of human psychology. In other words, they must work but, even more important, they must be trusted to work.

There are three key elements to Internet security. First, the need to keep messages private. Second, the need to prevent messages being corrupted or changed in transit – a requirement known as data integrity. Third, server and client authentication so that both ends of a transaction know they are talking to who they think they are talking to.

This is a fast-moving area and anything written now – particularly at a time of particularly intense development – is bound to be quickly outdated. So, to provide some lasting value, we will examine the current security offerings as exemplars rather than a statement of any stable and lasting position. We can at least gain a sense of the issues involved in designing such systems and get insight into the strategic direction that is being followed by the main players.

In early 1996, as these words are being written, there is a raft of compet-ing security systems becoming available, all implicitly or explicitly linked to facilitating secure payments so enabling Internet commerce to get off the ground. It is important to see that security in itself while crucial to payment mechanisms is essentially a thread that needs to run through them in order to facilitate a system that can be trusted by all its users. Trust is a key issue because technological reassurance is not enough – either for vendors or customers. This suggests that the eventual systems to dominate electronic commerce will be associated with well-established brands in the field of payments. It is no surprise and a great encouragement, therefore, to see such organisations as Visa, Mastercard, Mondex and many of the major clearing banks aligning themselves with the technology gurus of IBM, Microsoft, Netscape and other technology majors.

To gain a sense of these developments, however, we will start with the key issue of security itself and look, in particular, how one powerful and immediately available system works. We have already noted how Netscape has leveraged its secure socket layer (SSL) security technology to generate influence over the market for secure servers but the mechanism by which it offers good security is instructive and worth considering as a model of some of the more general issues important in this field. The SSL system is, of course, not the only player in the market. IBM has Internet keyed payments (iKP), Microsoft champions secure transaction technology (STT), browser giant Spyglass has its MD5 system and the US electronic trade specialists CommerceNet utilise Secure HTTP. There is considerable consolidation taking place among these proprietary offerings – Netscape and CommerceNet and other majors are, for example, collaborating through a joint venture called Terisa to create a single, common and open software standard to offer effective security on any server running the new software. However, Netscape's SSL is striking first because it is instantly available on hundreds, possibly thousands, of servers right now and also because it cunningly trades off inherent strength of security against other factors such as speed and cost.

The actual technology of SSL – like all security and payment systems – is arcane and complex, and we will gloss over the mathematic basis of what goes on for obvious reasons. With this in mind, the best way to understand how SSL operates is to imagine a real incident where a Web user with a Netscape browser visits a site offering transactional activities via a server running Netscape's secure server software.

When the server goes into secure mode, a message is flashed on the client's screen warning that the session now beginning between the browser and server will be protected by Netscape's SSL. This implies that all subsequent exchanges will be secure in the sense that the messages cannot be changed or examined by any agencies between the client and the server. There is a key symbol on all Netscape browser screens which denotes when exchanges are secure. Most of the time, it is a 'broken' key but when the browser is communicating with a secure server, the symbol is complete and unbroken. What is happening behind the scenes is technologically complex but conceptually very simple. When a secure transfer is needed, Netscape Navigator running on the client computer randomly generates a one-time token – usually a very large prime number – and this is subsequently used as the underlying mathematical basis for the encryption that will then be used to protect data during the secure session. It is important to understand that this token is used only once for the particular session in hand and has no other longer-term significance. In order for the server to use the token for encryption, it has to be communicated by the browser in a secure way. To do this, the client makes automatic contact with a trusted third party server known as a Certification Authority which holds details of what are called 'public keys' owned by all Netscape secure servers. In practice, this trusted position is currently held by the major US security firm RSA Data, the original creators of public key encryption systems. The client gains the public key of the server and uses this to encrypt the token before sending it to the server that it is communicating with. The server uses its secret, private key (a counterpart of the public one) to decrypt the token. The server and client then both use the token for SSL encryption and decryption during the session. At the end of the session, the token is discarded. The whole sequence of exchanges involving the keys and the encrypted token takes seconds and is transparent to the users.

The system goes one step further and allows the client to verify that the server with which it is communicating is the server it says it is and that it is not an impostor. This verification is accomplished by the client asking the server to encrypt a short private test message using its private key. The client then asks the Certification Authority to decrypt the message using the server's public key. If it works, the server is what it says it is. If it does not, then the server is an impostor. Again, the entire process is automatic and takes seconds.

The interesting element in this picture is the way SSL trades the strength of its encryption against other important factors such as speed and cost. Partly, however, Netscape is forced to use relatively weak encryption because strong encryption algorithms are classified by the US authorities as munitions and may not be exported outside the United States. The weakness of SSL is, however, only relative and it is quite good enough to survive all but the most determined attacks. However, its sacrifice of encryption strength makes it much cheaper for users and, equally import-ant, faster than any of its main competitors. The danger to its underlying security is cleverly minimised by ensuring that every encrypted session is based on a unique, once-only token. Even if the token is compromised by a breach in security all that is jeopardised is the single session and Netscape ensures that what is learned from decrypting the token is completely useless for decrypting any other tokens. The fraudsters would have to start all over again trying to figure out how to break the code. In other words, a single failure will contribute nothing to compromising any other secure sessions conducted by that browser–server or any other browser–server combination.

It is worth noting that SSL verifies the server's identity but does not check the client. This gap in the loop is now being closed by a digital signature technology developed by VeriSign, a spin-off company from RSA Data. The digital signature consists of two parts: a method of signing electronically that cannot be forged and a method of verifying that the signature was generated by the person it represents. The digital signature, of course, not only is vital to confirming identity in a secure transaction of the kind just described but also leads directly to the possibility of creating effective digital contracts and, in terms of payment systems, fully digital cheques or debit and credit advices. VeriSign's technology is soon to be incorporated in both Netscape's and Microsoft's browsers but is unlikely to remain unique. The underlying concept of the digital signature will soon be widely available and its impact on Web commerce will be huge as a component within trusted mechanisms.

Full payment mechanisms go further than security. As we saw in the imaginary transaction using SSL above, the security procedures merely protect information passing between client and server. For a secure payment process this is only the starting point. Transactions can, of course, be managed with nothing else. The server can request a credit card number, the client can send it and the server's proprietor can then manage the link with the credit card company in the same way as they might in a conventional, non-electronic transaction. The problem is that merchants hope to have hundreds of thousands of such transactions flowing through their servers every day and, in some cases, the transaction value may be quite small. The costs of managing this flow of vast numbers of, potentially, low value transactions are substantial and the prospect of an end-to-end system which takes transactions from servers through to their consummation with the relevant payment agencies such as credit card companies or banks is essential to establishing Web commerce on an effective and global basis.

There is also a security concern – more perceived than real but no less important because of it. When a credit card number is sent securely to a server, the server decodes it and makes it available to those managing the server. In other words, the merchant possesses the decrypted credit card information as indeed it must in order to process the transaction. In the real world, this situation is commonplace and universally accepted. However, in the electronic world, levels of insecurity are much higher among users. Even allowing merchants access to credit card numbers and protecting them fully on their way to merchants is not considered good enough.

As a result of this need to manage a perceived threat to customers, further security technologies have emerged to keep the client credit card numbers secret right up until the point they reach the credit card company. Netscape, for example, have developed software called Secure Courier which effectively seals the credit card information with a layer of encryption carried inside of SSL. When the encrypted information reaches the server, the SSL layer is stripped off leaving only the more deeply encrypted data. The merchant does not (cannot) decrypt this but instead adds to the encryption with further data about the sum of money involved in the transaction and the merchant's own identity. This encrypted information is then sent by the merchant the last mile to the credit card agency dealing with these transactions. The agency strips off the decrypted layers to get at both the merchant's and customer's data.

Even though the examples we are giving are specific proprietary offerings, we are now beginning to see the general key elements in an end-to-end payment system. But there is a further matter of deep concern. Everything we have outlined assumes that credit cards will be used as the basis of electronic commerce. To some extent, this is a natural and desirable way of seeing future payment systems. Credit cards are widely used, trusted and are supported by a well-developed and international infrastructure facilitating payments, customer billing and subscriber management. It would be foolish not to try to fuse electronic payment mechanisms with the world of credit cards. However, many people do not possess such cards and either prefer or are constrained by their credit ratings to deal in cash. In the record industry, for example, about 50 per cent of all products sold are sold for cash. A survey in the UK in 1995 showed that nearly 60 per cent of Britons preferred cash to cards. One way of addressing this problem would be to extend the payment systems to include direct debits of bank accounts but just as many people do not have credit cards there are also many who do not have bank accounts or would prefer not to debit them without being sure exactly what is in them to cover expenditure. Neither are credit cards or direct debits convenient for handling micropayments. Much Web commerce will want to depend on selling very high volumes of very low priced products or services. This could include the sale of access to content on a time basis measured in seconds or minutes leading to charges accumulating a few pence or cents, depending on where the server is located.

All this suggests the need for something that sounds deceptively simple. As well as credit card or bank-based debit mechanisms, there is a clear need for some form of digital money. Money is an excellent basis for trade so long as those using it can rely on it being genuine and also rely on the underlying promise of those supporting monetary systems that the money tokens can be converted among currencies and ultimately redeemed in terms of the value they purportedly represent. There are a number of electronic money initiatives already being promoted, the best known being Cyberbucks from the Amsterdam-based Cybercash. But while simple in concept, the idea founders because of lack of concerted international support by the government and financial institutions vital to giving digital cash its trusted underpinning. So far, therefore, digital cash looks like a distant prospect so far as genuinely pervasive influence is concerned and – despite their evident limitations – credit card and bank-based systems are likely to be the most widely available systems, at least until the turn of the century.

At the time of writing, there are about 30 schemes either suggested or under development to provide secure payment systems. Among the most promising are collaborations between Visa and Mastercard and moves by banking consortia in both the United States and Europe. The importance of these lies in the trusted nature of the partners. By 1997, the first of these mechanisms will be widely available and it is likely that the market will rapidly settle down into a handful of leading products all operating within a single agreed standard and all widely supported by current browser technologies. By the late 1990s, therefore, the catalyst for Web commerce will be in place and we will see an explosion in the use of the Web for all kinds of trading activities.

THE CHANGING FACE OF THE WEB

The conversion of the Web from being an arena for a few computer enthusiasts to a vast, sprawling environment filled with the bustle of commercial activity is not merely based on underpinnings such as security and payment mechanisms. The subjective experience of individuals using the Web is crucial to the pace and character of its future development.

Most times today the Web still seems a silent, infuriatingly slow and confusing place to visit. In fact, it is often such a dispiriting experience to surf the Web, it seems incredible that there is such widespread talk of the Web's creation as being almost on an equal footing in terms of global significance with the invention of digital computing. Is it really going to have such a revolutionary impact on our lives? The answer is yes, in time. But while the mainstream revolution is still – as this book is written – a (very) few years away, the seeds of revolution are everywhere to be seen. In coming years, the Web is going to change out of all recognition so far as the experience of existing, Webwise users are concerned. And by looking at what is about to happen for some of us we can get a sense for the kind of place the Web will soon become for all of us.

An important straw in the wind is the launch early in 1995 by Seattle-based Progressive Networks of RealAudio, a software package available free from its Web site. In the first year following its launch, nearly a million copies of the client software were distributed free and over 100 Web sites were offering RealAudio content. RealAudio works by compressing segments of an audio stream and sending it packet by packet from the server to the client computer. As the packets arrive they are buffered in the client memory, decompressed and then played back as soon as the buffer is full as a stream of sound. During playback, the buffering process continues in background to give the effect of a continuous stream. So far, quality on an ordinary dial-up connection at 14.4 kbs is, in radio broadcasting terms, a little below AM and in long continuous streams it is possible to hear occasional blips in the flow as each buffered segment is accessed. But it is a dramatically different experience from the traditional lengthy process of downloading files and playing them offline.

One of the earliest applications of RealAudio has been radio 'broadcasting'. From RealAudio's site you can access 24-hour Internet radio, which is based on the hourly output of news from ABC. The transmission is updated every hour and the previous 24 hours of programming is stored at the site. This means that what you hear is never more than a maximum of one hour later than its actual broadcast time and that you have access to all the news broadcast during the day in a true on-demand fashion. Clearly, this is still far from a real-time experience but the effect is almost as satisfying – particularly for European ears tuned in to the world of transatlantic radio for the first time. Elsewhere, music retailers and bands are also showing interest in the technology. The Rolling Stones are already making extensive use of RealAudio samples at their Voodoo Lounge site with unreleased extracts from some of their tours while elsewhere vendors are offering a try-before-you-buy option for cyberspace music shoppers.

Other RealAudio sites have quickly emerged including popular Korean songs from a site in Seoul, NTT-AD radio in Tokyo, Fox FM radio from Melbourne and scores of music, radio and magazine related sites based in North America. The only European sites so far are a Swedish national radio station, the Wildpark from Berlin, a fortune-telling service from London and radio services from the Open University at Milton Keynes in the UK and from a site in Milan, Italy.

Later in 1995, RealAudio was joined by a seemingly more powerful competitor which holds the prospect of real-time multimedia on the Web. US software specialist Xing Technology Corporation has announced a new generation of server software that promises to deliver real-time audio and video to ordinary dial-up users. For a lucky few, real-time video and audio are already there. The only drawback is that you need an ultra-fast connection to the fastest backbones of the Net in order to get the bandwidth you need. Very few people, for example, have the benefit of links to the US M-bone (an experimental multicast backbone system) or access to expensive high speed links such as T-lines. Xing claims it is going to change this situation dramatically with a new compression-based technology which will operate over conventional telephone lines.

Xing's new product is called Streamworks. Compatible with most existing Web browsers, it works over standard TCP/IP networks including, of course, the Internet itself. The engine driving Streamworks is a software implementation of MPEG which makes it possible to draw both video and audio from a server in real-time, allowing true on-demand access to multimedia content. The technology has already been proved in private business applications using fast lines. NBC's Desktop Video and Reuters Financial

Television, for example, both use the underlying server technology but send the data streams over private, fast TCP/IP networks to their customers.

The real breakthrough lies in the fact that the Streamworks implementation is designed for the World Wide Web and the considerably lower access speeds which commonly prevail. According to Xing, using an associated compression package in the server software, good quality audio can be delivered via an ordinary dial-up connection to the Internet via a 14.4 kbs modem. High quality audio is available through 28.8 kbs modems. With ISDN links Streamworks can, of course, do much better. Using the full 128 kbs available from two ISDN channels, Xing says that Streamworks can deliver in real-time, quarter screen video at 30 frames per second. Presumably frame speed can be traded against window size, enabling a bigger window to be used where there is little fast action in the video stream being delivered.

All that client computers need is Xing decompression software, which will soon be widely downloadable from a number of Web sites. With this in place, users will be able to use their browsers to access Streamworks sites wherever they emerge. Early interest – not surprisingly – is coming from radio stations. Radio Data Group – a subsidiary of EZ Communications, a US operator based in Washington State with 21 stations serving 8 national markets in its portfolio – has been the first to move. It has signed a deal with Xing to put live radio on the Web right away. The first stations to go live will be KMPS and KZOK serving the Seattle area. Michael Rau, president of Radio Data, reports that setting up an Internet broadcasting operation is straightforward and cheap. 'The operation of Xing software is very simple, much like the operation of a radio receiver,' Rau explains. 'When a hypertext link is selected, the radio station programme is instantly available and is the same programme material that is being broadcast at the time. It is not an audio file that needs downloading.... The operation is as simple as turning on a radio and selecting a station.'

Other radio companies are sure to follow but it is clear that non-traditional broadcasters may soon be setting up Xing sites too. So long as they have access to content, set-up costs are comparatively modest. At the time of writing, Xing's server software costs between $3,500 and $6,500 and is easy to configure and use. Client software can be downloaded free from Xing's own Web site. Registration – which buys full technical support and upgrade offers – currently costs a mere $29.

RealAudio and Streamworks are just examples. Many other systems like them are emerging and the trend is towards better, faster, cheaper 'good enough' multimedia. These developments are facets of the revolution now set to reshape our experience of the Web. Elsewhere, three dimensional images are also fast arriving. Virtual Reality Modelling Language (VRML), for example, is cheating the bandwidth restrictions of conventional dial-up access, enabling Web sites to create interactive 3D environments which can be accessed by dial-up connections. Here bandwidth limitations are thwarted by an ingenious technique which makes the client computer do the grunt work. In other words, only low resolution instructions are sent over the network. When these are received by a VRML compliant browser, the client computer builds the virtual world and provides the interactivity which generates the 3D application. Worlds Inc., for example, the US software company acquired in 1995 by UK media group, Pearson, has used an enhanced form of VRML to create a remarkable real-time chat environment that features 3D rooms and visual representations (known as avatars) of other simultaneous users of the system.

Perhaps most intriguing of all is the emergence of a new object-oriented programming language from Sun Microsystems, called Java. Java is a terse, secure, machine independent language which will increasingly be supported by major Web browsers. Sun has its own Java browser called HotJava but Netscape has also incorporated the technology in its new version of Navigator, ensuring that Java becomes a widely accessible language for most Web users. Java's fascination lies in its ability to send entire applications over the Net in compact bundles of code called applets (a contraction of the word 'application'). This makes it possible to send not only data but also an entire added value package containing, say, data and analysis and manipulation software to a Java compliant browser. In practical terms, Java effectively reshapes the potential of Web sites making them capable of delivering any application from a 3D animation sequence to support text in a Web document to a complete wordprocessing or spreadsheet application. It is also possible to continuously update an applet as it runs on a client machine. This makes it possible to stream real-time data like a conventional wire feed of news or financial information. If it can be written in Java it can be sent as an applet. Because Java is machine independent, target computers need only a simple Java viewer installed to gain access to whatever the applets contain. It is this reader technology which will soon be available in millions of browsers worldwide.

There are three important points about all of this remarkable development activity. First, we need to keep our feet on the ground. Java has a long way to go before it becomes a language in which applications can be built quickly and cheaply. All the other multimedia and 3D bells and whistles are compelling and seductive but cost money. At a time when the Web is still generating only modest revenues for its commercial pioneers, building all-singing, all-dancing sites is a big roll of the dice. Annual budgets are today increasingly numbered in millions, even tens of millions of dollars to build and maintain leading edge sites. While the power to transform the Web experience is being delivered fast, its use has to be wedded to the economic limitations of existing Web business models.

Second, and despite this cautionary note, the Web is clearly in the process of being transformed and our experience of it today is no guide to what it will be like in only a year's time. In other words, if we are building a Web strategy now – aside from economic housekeeping issues – it must not reflect the capabilities of the Web as it is today. We have to look ahead at the interactive, multimedia future.

Third, we need to understand this transformation as something which both changes the possible uses of the Web and the audience of users. Once the Web ceases to be the slow and silent place it is today and comes to life with sound, images and real-time interactivities which can be accessed via plain old telephone lines, it will attract an ever-widening demographic of users. Tomorrow's Web is truly everyone's Web.

CHAPTER 7

WHAT DOES IT ALL MEAN?

This is the ultimate, impossible question but one worth asking in spite of it being unanswerable. The immediate issue, of course, is who is asking because the answer will differ with differing agendas. We will examine some answers for only two communities: the world of content owners and originators – those who will ultimately drive the future offerings of the media industry in the new age – and the world of ordinary users and experiencers of media content. Each sit at extreme ends of a complex value chain. For commercial players, a key question will be where they sit in that value chain and how they should move to wield influence over those sectors most crucial to their own competitive advantage in whatever markets they target. The recipients of the outpourings of the media industry – digital or otherwise – have an equally pressing issue to confront. Where and how should they spend their media dollar? What product or, increasingly, which experience will most satisfy their needs? Ultimately, their decisions determine the future of the entire media industry and, within it, who will flourish and prosper and who will go to the wall.

As this suggests, digital media are not at heart a technological issue. This may be a curious thought with which to conclude a study of digital media, especially one which has offered so much commentary about technology. Nonetheless, it is a point worth making. In any consideration of digital media, we must, of course, focus on technology and its varied promises. However, we must never lose sight of a vital fact. It is people who design digital media systems and it is people who use them.

This has quite simple implications. Designers, developers and publishers of digital media offerings need to make a careful and accurate analysis of the human needs that their products are meant to address. Then they must translate their analysis into effective interface and product design. Although simple in essence, this notion is difficult to implement. True mastery of design and development in digital media – particularly in multimedia – demands more than an incremental change in existing established skills. It requires a genuine transformation or, perhaps, convergence. In the creation of effective digital products and services the professions of information scientist, designer, computer programmer, systems analyst, film maker, financier, and publisher must somehow be drawn together, either in a single extraordinary person or into a well-managed and effective creative team. By doing this we may begin to see products that people will want to buy and use.

We need to remember that however dazzling the technology may become, someone must be there to pay the bill. Digital media, like any technological advance, can be driven forward only by commercial success. This means addressing and meeting the needs of the people who will part with money for the products created for them. Ultimately, therefore, the real issue in digital media is not technology but the paying customer.

CONTENT IN THE DIGITAL WORLD

We have used the rather crude and ruffianly term 'content' throughout this book, so reducing the subtleties and richness of our literary, artistic and musical heritage to something that sounds uncomfortably like a commodity. It is well to emphasise, therefore, that content is a jargon term like any other but in this case intended to carry with it all the infinite shades of possibility that lie in the media resources which fuel education, information and entertainment in our daily lives. Even in the digital age, content is not – nor ever will be – a commodity. Value, however, will be added to the experience of content in myriad ways and, if anything, our already rich media heritage should become richer still thanks to the scope and power of digital technologies.

There is a catchy, much used phrase which gives us a starting point. It tells us that 'content is king'. In other words, however many new platforms and channels of delivery emerge and whatever the technological complexities underpinning them, the information highways and byways will be silent and empty without content to suffuse them and bring them to life. More than most gross over-simplifications, this one is dangerous. And it is dangerous because it contains an important grain of truth. It is evident and demonstrable that information delivery is meaningless without information to be delivered; that vehicles for education and entertainment will go nowhere without the content that educates and entertains. It is rather like admitting that 'I think, therefore I am' is really just another way of saying 'I think, therefore something must exist which does the thinking'. So in a very rudimentary sense content is surely king, because without it the media industry, and the increasingly digital infrastructure surrounding it, would simply have no substance. But clearly, the 'content is king' sentiment goes much further than games of logic. It contains a note of smug triumphalism. It really implies that content is the linchpin of the digital media industry and that for all the manoeuvrings of computing and communications companies, the key to the digital future – and, therefore, the strategic power determining that future – lies in the hands of those who own content.

There are a number of issues bound up in this. First, we have to be clear about whether the term 'content' in the digital media world means the same as it does in the old, analogue world. If it does not, then those who currently consider themselves well positioned as owners and administrators of important sources of content may find that their hands are filled with dust. Also, if the old understandings of content are defunct, then all the legal, regulatory and commercial infrastructure may well turn out to be, at best, inappropriate and, at worst, irrelevant.

WHAT IS DIGITAL CONTENT?

At its simplest, digital content means the forms of content that we understand in the analogue media world turned into bits and bytes so they can be manipulated, processed and transmitted by computer systems. As we saw earlier in this book, the commercial imperative of electronic publishing is to use the new digital format as a means of adding unique value to the underlying content which, in turn, can deliver new benefits to its users and commercial advantage to its publishers and distributors. This is stating the relatively obvious. What is more interesting is to consider whether the added values themselves create a new form of content or whether the needs of producing added value make unique calls on traditional content sources.

A trivial move from analogue to digital is the conversion of a text document from printed form to digital form so that it can be read from a computer screen. A few commercial products do little more than this and while commercially damned they at least fulfil the role of demonstrating how content can – if we want it to do so – pass quite undigested through the bowels of digital technology. In a case like this, the new form of content relates very closely to the old. But in more realistic cases of commercial development, the original content may be vastly more processed.

The obvious example is the use of content to build an online service. It is true that in much online exploitation the original content continues to exist in a recognisable form with the added values of searchability or updatedness helping to sell the transition to the digital form. But if we examine rising trends in Web site development, it is clear that a major genre of online publishing will rely on providing not content in its old sense but a content-based experience. Consider a typical Web site. If it is to be successful in attracting a constituency it is likely to be based on an interest area (rather than a pre-existing body of content). It is going to leverage substantial use of communications-based services such as forums, bulletin boards and real-time chat, which means that much of its content is going to be contributed by the site's users. It is going to be dynamic so that the overall content offering will change rapidly from moment to moment. It is also going to be increasingly personalised, so offering a distinctive one-to-one experience rather than a shared, generic one. Lastly, as technology makes it possible, the site will deliver multimedia, relying necessarily on a range of content types and related sources.

Whatever words we use to describe what this adds up to, we cannot be satisfied with merely the old sense of the word content. If we call such a Web site content-based, it must represent a new conception of content, governed largely by acknowledging that its uniqueness and power lies in delivering a compelling but varied and variegated experience to its users. In particular, the one-to-oneness that will increasingly become a feature of digital media products is especially distinctive. All existing content industries – broadcasting, music, film, publishing – are based on a generic model of distribution. In other words, their business is creating a single product and either replicating it in physical form and delivering it to as many individuals as they can find who will pay for it or transmitting it identically through a broadcasting infrastructure so that the same product is received by all who are tuned – or who have paid to be tuned – to the signal. In all these cases, the creators of the content products are driven by creative and commercial models which are tailored to the generic rather than the customised. In the digital domain, this generic model can persist – as we have seen in examples from the emerging world of digital broadcasting – but more importantly it can be disposed of entirely. To some extent, interactivity means every user can enjoy a slightly different content experience depending on how they choose to interact with a product but, more fundamentally, it means that information or entertainment experiences can be exactly tailored to individual needs and can be accessed when the user wants those experiences. In this situation, the substance of the content experience is determined more by the user than the supplier and a massive shift takes place in the balance of power between the two.

We have also implied that part of the new content experience on the Web will be multimedia. Indeed, it is clear that multimedia of some kind is a recurrent theme in both packaged and transmitted media. From the point of view of content development, the mere diversity of multimedia is enough to mark it out as fundamentally different from all previous forms of media. For the first time, it is possible to weave interactive experiences around a synthesis of all forms of media – sound, images and text – creating something unique in terms of the values it delivers but also unique in so far as the sourcing and editorialising of content is concerned. At its simplest, few if any traditional content companies will be able to source such diverse ingredients from their existing content assets. At a deeper level, the skills required to build products that successfully interpolate the different media forms within the envelope of a compelling experience for users are new and largely unprecedented.

What does this imply for the original boast that 'content is king'? First, it indicates that much depends on what is meant by 'content' and that traditional content companies may have much less to leverage in terms of content assets and content skills than perhaps they anticipate. Second – and by implication – there may be new generations of content originators and processors who can address the new markets as powerfully as the old players, in spite of the established brandings the oldsters may be able to bring to bear. If 'content is king', therefore, 'uneasy lies the head that wears the crown'.

WHOSE CONTENT IS IT, ANYWAY?

As we have seen, it is not safe to make smug assumptions about the continuing power of old content in the world of digital media. But we must accept that ownership of content remains a useful chip to possess in a game being played for increasingly high stakes. After all, whatever forms the eventual products take, someone's words, pictures and sounds will feature in it. This is really the mainspring of hope among traditional content companies also expressed by the 'content is king' mentality. The hope is that really content companies do not have to deal with modern-day techno-babble on its own terms. Ultimately, they hold the whole, incomprehensible circus to ransom by owning its lifeblood. Faced with the impenetrable, black arts of communications and computing, this is a reassuring notion to cling to. The reassurance, however, is often flawed by a simple fact. Content companies do not always own content.

Ownership itself is a difficult notion. It is based, of course, on the underlying idea of copyright which is a relatively well-understood legal and commercial concept. Where copyright is entirely owned, the rights position is clear. Ownership of copyright in a work of content implies ownership and therefore control of all rights. In general, however, life is not as simple as this implies. To gain a sense of the problems we will look at the position in just one content sector as an exemplar of the kinds of problems faced by them all. We will consider as our example the way in which a typical publishing company administers the content it commercialises and describe the bear traps that exist for the unwary.

Although some publishers either acquire copyright from authors or originate works via in-house, employed writers, most agree a licence with their authors. The licence agreement generally specifies that the publisher acquires 'volume rights' in the author's work. This means that the publisher can – during the legal term of copyright – embody the author's work as a book and produce and sell copies of it throughout a certain agreed territorial market and in an agreed language. Often this is as far as the principal rights conferred by such an agreement go. However, in a separate section dealing with what publishers term subsidiary rights, publishers are empowered to negotiate with third parties for further exploitations of the work. The revenue generated by these sub-licences are then shared between publisher and author. In some cases, certain forms of subsidiary rights are held back by the author or the author's agent but those commonly ceded to the publisher include serialisation rights, anthology rights, condensation rights, TV, radio and dramatic rights and the right to turn the basis of the work into a film. Increasingly, 'electronic rights' are being included in this section using a variety of wordings to try to capture all possibilities of electronic exploitation that might exist now or at some stage in the future.

At the level of definition alone, it is difficult to accurately frame an appropriate and safe subsidiary rights clause. 'Electronic rights' is not, for example, a term of art and needs reducing into unambiguous words which a court of law can make sense of. However, more fundamentally, even if the grant of subsidiary rights is properly framed, it does not give the publisher anything more than the right to negotiate with third parties to permit them to exploit the author's work. In other words, a subsidiary is a right not to exploit directly but only via a third party. This is important because it encapsulates a principle regulating the relationship with any content originator. Consider a bestselling author such as Wilbur Smith published in hardback by Macmillan. In a case like this, the publisher would be hard pressed to get anything more than the head right to produce the book. The rest would probably be retained by the author to allow his agent to do individual high value deals for the subsidiary exploitations. But imagine for a moment that he had allowed Macmillan to negotiate film rights on his behalf. If Macmillan has a good track record of hunting down interest among the studios or independent production companies and driving a hard bargain, there may be nothing unusual or surprising about this. However, imagine instead if Macmillan wanted to exploit those selfsame rights itself. Instead of merely wishing to negotiate with third parties, it decided it wanted to make the movie itself. It is not hard to imagine the author's reaction. What does Macmillan know about making and distributing movies? Where is its track record in this field and when and how will it exploit the rights it is now seeking?

Clearly, this is an unlikely scenario but it is exactly analogous to publishers trying to shift electronic rights out of their subsidiary rights portfolio and into their head rights. Authors with any commercial acumen – and these would tend to be just the kind that are relevant – would ask the same questions Wilbur Smith would ask about Macmillan's ambitions in the movie industry. So you want to acquire electronic rights? What kinds of exploitations do you plan? How will you implement them? When will you implement them? And, by the way, can you demonstrate any competence or track record in electronic publishing? In other words, publishers without electronic publishing experience under their belt will find it difficult to gain direct access to the electronic rights of their author's works. But without access to those rights, they will never gain electronic publishing experience. A classic Catch-22.

The insecurity of publishing rights over electronic exploitations goes much further than the work provided by the author's efforts. Illustrated books, for example, will use images drawn from a wide range of proprietary sources. Some will be owned (or administered) by picture agencies, others by the author and some may be commissioned by the publisher from third party photographers. Usually, if a publisher is intent on only producing a book, the permissions garnered for this collateral copyright material covers the right only to reproduce it in book form in certain, defined territories for the life of the particular edition of the book. In other words, glamorously illustrated books which look the perfect basis for a multimedia adaptation may instead be a nightmare of new – and highly expensive – rights clearances in order to produce, say, a CD-ROM title.

In practice, the precise position concerning what a publisher does or does not own and the degree of control it has over its publishing assets is immensely variable and is ultimately determined by the minutiae of countless contracts defining relationships between content originators such as authors, artists, photographers and designers and publishing companies of all kinds. Even outright ownership of copyright is often not a complete solution to the problems of electronic publishing development. The UK non-fiction specialist Dorling Kindersley, for example, has always ensured that it owns copyright in almost every word and image it publishes. This policy was in place long before electronic media emerged and is now paying dividends by facilitating the company's shift to becoming a major multimedia publisher. But even Dorling Kindersley – with all its copyright assets – is finding that it still has to license or originate vast amounts of new image and audio material to support multimedia development.

Even at a technical level, copyright ownership does not necessarily grant the publisher unfettered rights to exploit the content concerned. In Europe, to varying degrees, originators' rights can persist even after the assignment of copyrights in their work. The legal concept of moral rights means that in most European territories, originators have the right both to be identified with their work – known as the moral right of paternity – and the right to prevent their work receiving 'derogatory treatment' – the moral right of integrity. It is not clear what is meant by derogatory treatment but it is plain that interactive products take the control of how content is treated increasingly away from content companies and place it in the hands of individual end users. This notion, after all, lies at the heart of the digital revolution. There exists, therefore, some risk that the originators of content could sue its exploiters long after assigning away their copyrights. Currently, the degree of risk is unclear and is largely confined to Europe and soon Australasia. But it is an important reminder that even ownership of copyright does not confer a carte blanche for the exploitation of content, particularly in the dangerous waters of interactive media. Even in the United States where moral rights are not recognised, the multimedia industry must take careful note of their implications. The process of law is enforced in the territory in which a breach occurs. This means that a US publisher is vulnerable to suits for breach of moral rights in any territory that recognises them. As exports to Europe become an increasingly important commercial avenue for US players, they will have to be cautious about their use of content when they exploit it in key European markets.

This is merely a swift and broadbrush overview of some of the issues surrounding content ownership. While we have not explicitly examined the film, TV and music industries, comparable – sometimes identical – issues pervade all media and information sectors. At a technical level alone, they are daunting but at an operational level they are often disastrous. In far too many media organisations, simple issues of contractual housekeeping have long been neglected so that documents that should unambiguously define the relationship between content company and the content it seeks to exploit are often vague, confusing and even misleading. Coupled with naïve judgements about what those documents really imply, the rights position of many content companies – including some of the largest in the world – is a minefield of legal disasters waiting to happen. It is not surprising that the most vital starting point for any electronic publishing strategy, therefore, is a thorough audit of a company's contractual rights over its supposed assets.

NEW CONTENT OR OLD?

The problems of identifying ownership in content is complex and vital so long as we intend or hope to leverage what already exists in new electronic exploitations. If we decide to start from scratch and originate new content either for a particular electronic development or – commercially more sensible – for a range of conventional and electronic exploitations, we can at least build up our control of the content assets in a consistent and considered way. There are still challenging technical issues in the drafting of related agreements and the gathering of expert legal guidance, while never cheap, is a vitally important investment to make. No corners can be cut but the potential outcome is a clear map of content ownership in a product or range of products and the ability to sleep soundly at night thereafter.

It is important, however, to consider the question of originating new content from a strategic point of view as well as a technical one. The overwhelming temptation to which the entire digital media industry has largely succumbed is to approach product development by referring to what existing assets can be leveraged. Publishers comb their lists for books with strong enough branding or content attributes to make good CD-ROM or online products. Television and film companies examine their portfolios for gems. And music companies wonder how best to generate new revenue from their backlist repertoires. There is nothing inherently wrong about this emphasis so long as it driven in the right way. What really counts is whether the impetus to examine current assets is shaped by an appreciation of the needs of the market rather than a compulsion to find ways of building new products out of old because the old products performed so well in their own analogue niches. In other words, content companies have to be market facing. This may seem too obvious to state. But the reality is that many operate on hunch and instinct. The approach works sometimes but is a recipe for disaster when applied to new high investment product adventures.

Being market facing is tough. It takes courage, particularly because the answers the market gives to your probing may not be the ones you wish to hear. The market may decide, for example, that none of your existing content or brand assets is suited to electronic exploitation and that if you wish to play in the new markets you will have to reinvent and diversify your business. Or the market may indicate that your brand is powerful but that the underlying content attached to the brand needs such deep adaptation that electronic publishing becomes tantamount to reoriginating all that you have hitherto created. The vital need to listen to the market is the oldest lesson that the world of commerce has to teach us but, for a variety of reasons and in a variety of ways, content companies wishing to play in the new digital media markets have partly or completely ignored its universal message.

It is not a simple matter to identify the voice of the market although classic research techniques such as surveys, focus groups and pilot products are all useful starting points. Most powerfully, however, the market can be heard in its myriad responses to existing media and to the new generation of interactive products and services. For example, it is clear that running different CD-ROMs – each of which make small but different adjustments to a PC's system software – can cause conflicts within a user's machine resulting in the longer term in knock-on problems for a whole range of other applications. Yet few titles reassure users – many do not even work properly or they contain worrisome bugs. The message of the market which is deafeningly obvious is that it wants CD-ROM products that load and operate consistently, reliably and without disturbing the equilibrium of the machine on which they run. Not merely products that work – a blindingly obvious conclusion – but products that convey strong trust at a technical as well as creative level. Similarly, if we look at the judgement of the market in the world of online services, we see that users above all else enjoying using online services for communication. The message therefore is to strand communications-based experiences within an overall online offering. By contrast, some companies are merely trying to shift their real world business sideways into cyberspace. Taking publishing as our example once again, book publishers are tending to see the online world as just another opportunity to sell books. It may well be – but the message of the market-place is that online users want much more from their experiences than access to a publisher's catalogue or to the cyber equivalent of a bookstore.

This puts the position bluntly and with some exaggeration to make a point. But even if we wish to refine and tune the argument, the overwhelming issue is plain. Commercialising the digital media market-place starts where all markets start: with the needs and desires of the paying customer.

STRATEGIES FOR EXPLOITING CONTENT

There are three options for content companies and while each can be followed independently, most electronic media strategies are an interplay among all of them:

- Licensing
- Joint ventures
- Going it alone

LICENSING

First, content can license its assets to third parties and step back from direct exploitation altogether. There are a raft of complex issues determining how best to handle a licensing strategy but it is generally understood as a low risk route to added value revenues. It is not, however, a 'no risk' route even though a third party is assuming the investment and marketing load. A bad product created by a poorly performing licensee can do untold and irreparable harm to the future electronic prospects of a content asset. This is particularly true for high profile, crown jewel assets where failure, if it occurs, occurs in the full glare of the public eye. The message is more than merely to choose partners carefully, it is to choose then monitor carefully and – despite the distance introduced by licensing – to be continuously involved with the quality control of the product and the marketing plans surrounding it.

Defining the nature of the rights granted is also a fundamental and non-trivial task. Time plays a role here, particularly since both technology and terminology is so fast-changing. In the early 1980s, some licensors permitted contracts meant to confer video disc rights to describe them as 'optical disc' rights. If the term of the agreements had been a few years, no damage would have been done. But some such contracts endured for ten years, long enough for 'optical disc rights' to embrace (arguably) the whole raft of CD-ROM based platforms. Even in the late 1980s, when CD-ROM was an established reality, the danger remained. Rights granted which did not clearly specify the operating system of particular platforms to be included in the grant, risked being interpreted as giving away rights to every CD technology in existence or thereafter invented! Short terms, therefore, make sense for licensors if only to allow them to escape from dreadful contractual bungles. But it makes less sense to licensees who need a reasonable contractual period to recoup their own investments and make commercial sense of the deal. The lesson is an important and general one in rights licensing. It is always possible to spell out the technical issues relevant to both parties but, to conclude a deal, there must be a meeting of minds over the commercial logic of the agreements reached.

Assessing the value of any given licence is a vital but immensely difficult task. In an industry where there are few established norms it would be easy for licensors to put their tongues firmly in their cheeks and bargain for as much as they can get while prospective licensees do the same but try to pay as little as possible. The mature reality is that the terms of the deal must ultimately be equitable. And an equitable deal has to be based on a realistic assessment of the value which each party brings. Content clearly has worth but so does the value to be added by a multimedia publisher through collateral content, interactive programming and access to the market. Ultimately all deals can be measured by this interplay of relative valuations of contributions.

It is clear, of course, that strongly branded content, in particular, is in high demand and that brand in itself can confer substantial – even over-whelming – value. There is no doubt about the reason. As the platforms and channels of delivery multiply, users of media and information – the paying customers – increasingly need guidance and reassurance to aid their choices. They need trusted advisers and brands have long played that role in the real world and can do so again in the digital one. Indeed, branding can be so cherished by electronic publishers that the value or extent of the underlying content supporting that brand may become secondary. A few years ago, for example, multimedia publisher Grolier Interactive acquired CD-ROM rights to the *Guinness Book of Records*. It paid a substantial upfront royalty not merely because Guinness had an interesting database to trade but because the name of the *Book of Records* is one of the most widely recognised in the world. In other words, Grolier paid a premium for a pre-existing franchise which it could then leverage – even at the cost of funding substantial additional content to support a multimedia pro-duction – successfully in the CD-ROM market-place. For Guinness Pub-lishing the deal made good sense so long as it did not lock up the rights for too long a period: the term of the licence was crucial both because strategies and the value of licences change. A consumer CD-ROM licence negotiated at the end of the 1980s would hardly command huge value simply because practically no consumer market existed at that time. A few years later, however, the story looked very different. In other words, granting rights for short periods, as we noted above, is an essential element in licensing strategy in sectors where markets and technologies are changing fast. In another sense too, it was important for Guinness to be able to reclaim its rights in a relatively short period. In the early 1990s, when it licensed Grolier, its strategy was confined to licensing – it had no interest in becoming more directly involved in digital media markets. But by the time the licence expired, the company's management had changed and its strategy had become vastly more proactive. It now looks as if the *Guinness Book of Records* will be exploited directly by its publisher, either independently or in joint venture.

Joint ventures

Licensing will probably form a part of every content company's strategy because the company will always possess elements of content of value to potential licensees and licensing of it need not – if handled wisely – conflict with the company's more proactive ambitions in the new markets. Apart from its technical complexity, however, licensing is not a good way, taken on its own, of gaining substantial experience of new markets. For most companies with serious interests in electronic publishing, therefore, joint ventures designed to spread risk and create an effective portfolio of business strengths often make the most obvious and immediate sense in strategic terms. This is not the place to deal in detail with structuring joint ventures but we can at least touch upon the underlying question of choosing partners. After all, if the appropriate commercial strengths are not leveraged in the first place, the issue of correct structuring is barely relevant because the joint venture will fail at the first hurdle.

Sometimes successful joint ventures are created through happenstance meetings of companies in different sectors who find almost by accident that there is convergence in their objectives and synergy in their business strengths. However, more commonly the best marriages are not made in heaven but worked at in a professional and committed fashion. The objectives governing a choice of partners are largely shaped by an assessment of the strengths that are needed to form an effective partnership. Those strengths are fairly clear: access to content, content skills and technological knowhow, and appropriate marketing muscle and secure, long-term access to market. Beyond this bedrock, the permutations are endlessly varied. Content companies may partner with other content companies to draw together the diverse range of materials (and, possibly, brandings) needed for multimedia products. Distribution companies may be wooed to create a secure pipe for marketing efforts. And technical knowhow may be brought in to ensure deep control over effective product-building processes. What ultimately decides the quality of the joint venture is whether the partnerships provide a powerful enough synergy to give the outcome of the effort a strong competitive advantage. They also need to work at a human level so chemistry and culture are also ingredients that cannot be neglected.

Sometimes obvious-seeming alliances do not work well in practice because the reality is that the benefits conferred are unequally shared. For example, in 1995 a leading European distributor of packaged media products (audio CDs, books, computer games and videos) called Total Home Entertainment (THE) acquired a multimedia entertainment publisher called FunSoft. About a year later, leading US direct marketeer CUC International bought educational multimedia publisher Davidson & Associates and games publisher Sierra On-line. In both cases, the deals made excellent sense for the two content companies for whom access to market was vital at a time when distribution channels were dangerously congested with too much product chasing too little shelf space. For the multimedia publishers, downstreaming themselves towards distribution, retail and ultimately the end users themselves had a powerful commercial logic. For the distribution companies, however, the deals made little sense. While they gained secure access to content, this hardly offered them value at a time when they and all their colleagues in the distribution and retail sectors were being pursued by thousands of content sources, every one of them yearning for some bandwidth to gain access to market. Worse, the deals distracted the distributors from their core competencies into new and unfamiliar business territory. In other words, in the packaged media world, content downstreaming itself for distribution makes good sense; distribution upstreaming itself for content makes none.

Importantly, this kind of mismatch in partnering does not necessarily apply if you transfer the same alliance structures to the online world. Here distribution – or online access provision which is the closest analogue to the notion of distribution as it exists in the packaged media world – is rapidly being commoditised and it is going to be increasingly difficult for the main players to leverage business value simply out of providing online users with access to online environments. There have to be other strings to their strategic bow. For some, as we have seen, offering access remains a means – if properly managed – of owning customers with all that implies for long-term commercial advantage. This is the game being played by Internet access providers such as AT & T, Microsoft and MCI. Others see the future in providing access but directing it towards content in which they have a stake. Here is where distribution and content combine well online in a way they do not offline. This is why proprietary majors such as America Online and Prodigy are busy investing in joint ventures with content companies. They want a stake in the revenues derived from Web sites at which they will point their constituencies. Of course, the majors do not play a single game and the reality is that distribution and content online is forming a variety of marriages, all of which are designed, one way or another, to leverage strategic influence and competitive advantage.

Joint venturing therefore, merely at the level of building intelligent partnerships, is complex. Structuring the deal thereafter is also challenging. Key issues are frequently overlooked or mismanaged. In the multimedia field, a classic blunder is for partners to co-operate in creating a new product made by fusing their joint skills and assets without defining who owns the outcome of all their efforts! Another related howler is to forget to determine what happens to the assets (including revenue flows) created by the joint venture after it has ended. Such detailed structural issues are numerous and beyond the scope of this book. The brief points made here, however, are intended to illustrate just a few key issues so that joint venturers are better prepared for the fray when they enter it.

GOING IT ALONE

The third option for content companies is to invest directly and independently in electronic publishing. This is generally an expensive, high risk option which – in consumer markets particularly – requires confidence and consummate business skill. Above all, going it alone needs a firm commitment to a clear and ongoing understanding of markets, product-building processes and the ways in which the digital media world is changing and developing, almost on a moment-by-moment basis. It is, of course, possible to tackle this strategic option like a mouse nibbling a piece of cheese – particularly in low volume, high priced market sectors – and wherever possible such caution is admirable as a means of building expertise while simultaneously minimising business risk. The danger in a modest piecemeal approach is always that too little will achieve nothing of substance in terms of gaining expertise, establishing brand profile in electronic markets or generating sufficient revenue flows and margin to feed the vision and ambition of top management.

THE VISION THING

While everyone involved in the emerging digital media industry needs to keep their feet firmly on the ground, there is also an urgent need for vision, particularly among the captains of commercial enterprise. There are plenty of foot soldiers ready to evangelise the future potential of digital media but too few top managers capable of real and sustained insight into the opportunities and threats of a fast-changing market-place. Without their commitment, corporate activity will become aimless, misdirected and ultimately self-defeating. But such commitment needs a quality of belief and foresight. Not, of course, in a specific, well-defined future but in a landscape vision of where broad trends of development are taking us. But such vision, in spite of its broad canvas, needs to be focused accurately. And accuracy implies a base of knowledge and understanding rooted in the events of today that are driving and shaping the business environment of tomorrow. In other words, vision thrives only on comprehension, a realisation of implications and significances. This means that vision must be founded on finding out, among all the myriad events of the day, what matters and what does not. Because change is taking place at breakneck speed and the processes of change are still accelerating; because the inter-actions of the digital media industry now involve a convergence of many different industry sectors; because the meaning of change is often obscured by difficult, even incomprehensible technologies; and because the control-ling brains of major business are (quite rightly) immensely busy tending their core assets: commitment to gaining insight and understanding which is, in turn, capable of accurately informing strategic plans, implies a sub-stantial investment of time, money and corporate will. The real vision required, therefore, is the vision to see that the investment must be made. There is no alternative.

All of this implies that vision must be constrained by the imperatives of business. While we have persistently argued that the commercialisation of digital media is the principal engine of development, there is thankfully room for a human dimension too. All of us involved in building the new media industry, and changing the old, are attracted by the excitement not merely of a revenue opportunity but of a tool to change the way that human beings experience the world. None of us can see clearly where even the next decade will take us in terms of our access to education, information and entertainment but there are few true believers in the digital media future who do not hope that as well as generating an industry, all our efforts will succeed in bringing people across the world together in mutual understanding, appreciating differences but stressing commonalities. The most important human vision, therefore, is that our whole global com-munity – both the possessed and the dispossessed – can share equally in a rich future of media, information and global communications that will ultimately make our lives and the lives of our children richer and more meaningful.

INDEX